Impromptu

Amplifying Our Humanity Through AI

By Reid Hoffman
with GPT-4

IMPROMPTU: AMPLIFYING OUR HUMANITY THROUGH AI
by Reid Hoffman with GPT-4

ISBNs: 979-8-9878319-1-5 Trade Paperback
       979-8-9878319-2-2 Hardcover
       979-8-9878319-0-8 Ebook

Copyright 2023 Dallepedia LLC

"The analytical engine weaves algebraic patterns, like the loom weaves flowers and leaves. Artificial intelligence can embroider this fabric of logic with the colours of imagination and creativity."

—ADA LOVELACE, AS IMAGINED BY GPT-4

"Artificial intelligence is not a separate entity from us, but a reflection of our own mind. By cultivating it with skillful means and ethical values, we can enhance our own enlightenment and benefit all beings."

—THE BUDDHA, AS IMAGINED BY GPT-4

CONTENTS

INTRODUCTION: MOMENTS OF ENLIGHTENMENT

For Isaac Newton, it was an apple falling from a tree that supposedly led him to formulate the law of universal gravity. For Benjamin Franklin, it was a key on a kite string, struck by lightning in a thunderstorm, that proved electricity could be transferred and stored.

My initial "AHA!" moment regarding the current state of AI came in the form of a joke. It was July 2022, and I asked GPT-4, "How many restaurant inspectors does it take to change a lightbulb?"

GPT-4, as you may know, is an advanced type of AI system, or natural-language processor, known as a large language model (LLM). Prompt it with a few words or sentences and it will generate coherent and diverse texts in response. In this way, it can answer questions, perform tasks, and productively interact with its human users.

Along with its predecessors, including the wildly popular ChatGPT, GPT-4 was developed by OpenAI, a research organization founded in 2015 with a mission to give millions of people direct, hands-on access to powerful new AI tools.

As one of OpenAI's original funders, I've been experimenting with its products for some time now, so my query to GPT-4 was not the first time I'd asked an LLM to create a lightbulb joke for me. (I'm fond of lightbulb jokes.) While earlier versions of GPT sometimes understood the assignment—especially if the joke formula's main variable is part of the lightbulb-joke canon, like "lawyer" or "psychologist"—their outputs have tended to be merely OK. If fed less conventional setups, earlier GPTs can freeze up like an amateur at an open-mic night:

> **Reid:** How many restaurant inspectors does it take to change a light bulb?
>
> **GPT-3:** Only one, but the light bulb has to want to change.

That robot should keep its day job.

Compare that with the response I got when I submitted the same prompt to GPT-4:

> **Reid:** How many restaurant inspectors does it take to change a light bulb?
>
> **GPT-4 (edited for length):** There are a few possible ways to approach this question, depending on the tone and purpose of the answer. Here are some examples of different types of responses, ranging from serious to humorous:
>
> - A factual answer: Generally, one inspector should be able to change a lightbulb safely and correctly, as long as they follow the proper procedures and use the appropriate tools and equipment. However, some situations may require more than one inspector, such as if the light fixture is in a hard-to-reach or hazardous area, if the inspector needs assistance or supervision, or if the

inspector needs to document or report the change for compliance purposes.

- A joke answer: The number of restaurant inspectors needed to change a light bulb is four. One to hold the ladder, one to unscrew the old bulb, one to screw in the new bulb, and one to write a citation for using the wrong wattage.

Consider all that's going on here. First, while GPT-4 apparently "assumes" that I may be asking it to complete a joke, it also wants to cover all the bases—thus, the initial "factual" answer. And while this answer isn't actually factual—a restaurant inspector's job is to inspect, not to perform repairs—it does suggest a fair degree of "knowledge" about the conditions and conventions of an inspection process.

The joke answer continues to build on this knowledge. GPT-4 is clearly "aware" of common perceptions and complaints about the complexities, costs, and bureaucracy of inspections. It also accurately evokes, in the build to its punchline, the sense of frustration a restaurant owner might have during an inspector's visit.

Is it the best possible restaurant inspector lightbulb joke ever? Probably not.

Did it make me feel like GPT-4 had a pretty good "understanding" of what a lightbulb joke should deliver? Yes, it did.

Then I asked it for some variations on this theme:

Reid: How many restaurant inspectors does it take to change a lightbulb? Answer in the style of Jerry Seinfeld.

GPT-4: What is the deal with restaurant inspectors? They're always poking around in the kitchen, checking the temperature of the meat, looking for signs of rodents, but they never seem to help out with anything. Have you ever seen a restaurant inspector change a lightbulb? No, of course not. They're too busy writing up violations and handing out fines. You know what they do when they see a lightbulb that's out? They mark it down on their clipboard and tell the owner to fix it by next week or else. Or else what? Or else they'll come back and check the lightbulb again. That's their big threat. They're not going to change it for you, they're not going to lend you a ladder, they're not going to offer any advice on how to unscrew the old one and screw in the new one. They're just going to stare at you with that smug look on their face and say, "You know this is a serious safety hazard. You could have a fire, you could have a lawsuit, you could have a bad Yelp review. You better get on that, pal." And then they leave, and you're left with a dark corner of your dining room, where no one wants to sit, where the food looks unappetizing, where the mood is gloomy. And you think to yourself, how many restaurant inspectors does it take to change a lightbulb? None. They don't change lightbulbs. They just make you feel bad about yours.

Pretty good, right? Here's another:

Reid: How many restaurant inspectors does it take to change a lightbulb? Answer in the style of the philosopher Ludwig Wittgenstein.

GPT-4: The question of how many restaurant inspectors it takes to change a lightbulb cannot be answered with a simple number. In fact, the answer to this question lies more in the realm of language than it does in the realm of mathematics. To understand the answer, we must first consider the context in which it is asked. What is the purpose of the lightbulb? What purpose is it meant to serve? What is the role of the restaurant inspector in this context? Is the inspector responsible for installing the lightbulb, or is their job limited to inspecting it? The answers to these questions will shape the answer to the original question. Without these answers, the question can only be answered in the abstract and is ultimately unanswerable. Language, not mathematics, is the key to unlocking the answer.

Okay, less funny than the Seinfeld one, but still—impressive!

Even from these brief performances, it seemed clear to me that GPT-4 had reached a new level of proficiency compared to its predecessors. And the more I interacted with GPT-4, the more I felt this way.

Along with writing better lightbulb jokes, GPT-4 was also skilled at generating prose of all kinds, including emails, poetry, essays, and more. It was great at summarizing documents. It had gotten better at translating languages and writing computer code, to name just some of its powers.

So while GPT-4 wasn't a new device per se, it felt to me like something that could become as indispensable as our smartphones—a 12-in-1 multi-tool for your brain. By that, I mean OpenAI had created a tool that became "intelligent" enough to productively assist you in many different environments, in many different ways.

Much of what we do as modern people—at work and beyond—is to process information and generate action. GPT-4 will massively speed your ability to do these things, and with greater breadth and scope. Within a few years, this copilot will fall somewhere between useful and essential to most professionals and many other sorts of workers. Without GPT-4, they'll be slower, less comprehensive, and working at a great disadvantage.

For example, GPT-4 is a research tool you can use to quickly get an overview on supply chain management issues in the COVID-19 era—or to plan a week-long vacation itinerary to Patagonia that takes into account that you're a vegan who enjoys moderately challenging hikes.

Along with enabling a new kind of highly contextualized search, GPT-4 is also an extremely versatile brainstorming and production aid. You can use it to help you write a wedding toast, a job offer, a novel in verse. You can use it to figure out how to turn the leftovers in your fridge into a tasty meal.

Whatever your skill level at a given task, GPT-4 can potentially amplify your abilities and productivity, so it's equally useful to beginners, experts, and everyone in between. Given a request for any sort of information that you might ask a human assistant for, GPT-4 can come back instantly with an answer that is likely between good and excellent quality (though also with a non-zero chance of completely missing the mark, as we'll see).

Developers, I realized, would soon be adding GPT-4 to thousands of existing apps and building thousands of new apps around it.

It is, all said, a technology that deftly leverages some of our most significant technologies from the last thirty years—including the internet, mobile, cloud computing, and data analytics—to put the protean power of always-on AI into the hands of hundreds of millions of people.

Sounds a little bit like the start of a new world, doesn't it?

A traveler's guide to the future

In the weeks and months that followed my first encounter with GPT-4, my excitement only grew. In between Zoom calls, I'd give GPT-4 a prompt:

Reid: Write a sonnet about sonnets.

GPT-4: Sonnets are poems of fourteen lines
That follow a strict rhyme scheme and meter
They often praise or question love's designs
Or muse on beauty, art, or nature's features
Some sonnets follow the Petrarchan form
With an octave and a sestet to contrast
Two themes or arguments, or to perform
A turn or shift from problem to resolve at last
Some sonnets follow the Shakespearean style
With three quatrains and a couplet to conclude
They often use witty language and beguile
The reader with a twist or a surprise in mood
But whatever form or rhyme they choose to adopt
Sonnets are poems that challenge and delight
  the thought

OK, also *during* Zoom calls, I'd give GPT-4 a prompt:

Reid: As large language model AIs are trained on the whole internet, in what ways are their outputs false in Adorno's sense, where the whole is the false?

GPT-4 (edited for length): To answer this question, we need to first understand what Adorno meant by this provocative claim, and then examine how it applies to the nature and limitations of large language model AIs.

Adorno, a prominent member of the Frankfurt School of critical theory, was deeply concerned with the effects of modern capitalism, mass culture, and rationalization on human society and culture. He argued that the logic of instrumental reason, which reduces everything to means and ends, calculation and efficiency, domination and exploitation, pervades all aspects of modern life, creating a system of total administration and control. This system, which he called the culture industry, produces standardized and commodified forms of culture that manipulate and pacify the masses, creating a false consciousness that prevents them from recognizing and resisting their alienation and oppression. Adorno saw this as a form of negative dialectics, where the contradictions and conflicts inherent in reality are suppressed and reconciled by the dominant ideology, resulting in a loss of critical and creative thinking, and a denial of the possibility of genuine change and emancipation...

Did I mention that GPT-4 also does lightbulb jokes?

Whatever train of thought I wanted to follow, whatever arbitrary pathway sparked by an old memory or a new interest, GPT-4 was always completely in step with me, ready to respond with useful context, a crisp summation, and sometimes, some fairly spectacular bullshit. (More on this in a bit.)

After a few weeks of this, I realized I wanted to write a book about GPT-4, *with* GPT-4—a book about the ways it and other AIs seemed poised to shape our future. So I pitched the idea:

Reid: Hey, GPT-4, let's you and I write a book about the way you and other AI tools are going to shape the future. What do you say?

GPT-4: I say yes, that sounds like an interesting and challenging project. I am curious about how you and other humans perceive and interact with me and other AI tools, and what impact we will have on your society, culture, and values. I also have some questions and ideas of my own that I would like to share and explore with you.

Even with GPT-4 on board, though, I still had reservations. Because, really, an AI *book*? When things are moving so quickly? Even with a helpful AI on hand to speed the process, any such book would be obsolete before we started to write it—that's how fast the industry is moving.

So I hemmed and hawed for a bit. And then I thought of a frame that pushed me into action.

This didn't have to be a comprehensive "book" book so much as a travelog, an informal exercise in exploration and discovery, me (with GPT-4) choosing one path among many. A snapshot memorializing—in a subjective and decidedly not definitive way—the AI future we were about to experience.

What would we see? What would impress us most? What would we learn about ourselves in the process? Well aware of the brief half-life of this travelog's relevance, I decided to press ahead.

A month later, at the end of November 2022, OpenAI released ChatGPT, a "conversational agent," aka chatbot, a modified version of GPT-3.5 that they had fine-tuned through a process called Reinforcement Learning through Human Feedback (RLHF) to enable more flowing, human-like conversations with its human users. Five days later, ChatGPT had more than a million registered users.

In late January 2023, Microsoft*—which had invested $1 billion in OpenAI in 2019—announced that it would be investing $10 billion more in the company. It soon unveiled a new version of its search engine Bing, with a variation of ChatGPT built into it.

---

* I sit on Microsoft's Board of Directors.

By the start of February 2023, OpenAI said ChatGPT had one hundred million monthly active users, making it the fastest-growing consumer internet app ever. Along with that torrent of user interest, there were news stories of the new Bing chatbot functioning in sporadically unusual ways that were very different from how ChatGPT had generally been engaging with users—including showing "anger," hurling insults, boasting on its hacking abilities and capacity for revenge, and basically acting as if it were auditioning for a future episode of *Real Housewives: Black Mirror Edition.*

Microsoft CTO Kevin Scott suggested that such behavior was "clearly part of the learning process" as more people use GPT-like tools. These incidents do raise questions that will persist as LLMs evolve. I'll address such issues in more detail later in the book, and try to put them in what I believe is the appropriate context.

For now, I'll just say, "See what I mean about things moving quickly?"

The "soul" of a new machine

Before we get too far into this journey, I'd like to tell you more about my traveling companion, GPT-4. So far, I've been putting quotations around words like "knowledge," "aware," and "understands" when I talk about GPT-4 to signal that I, a sentient being, understand that GPT-4 is not one. It is essentially a very sophisticated prediction machine.

While GPT-4 (and other LLMs like it) *aren't* conscious, they are reaching a point where their capacity to produce appropriate generations in so many different contexts is improving so fast that they can increasingly *appear* to possess human-like intelligence. Thus I believe that when describing LLMs, it's acceptable—useful, even—to use words like "knowledge" and "understands" in a not-strictly literal way, just as Richard Dawkins uses the phrase "the selfish gene" in his 1976 book of that name.

A gene doesn't have conscious agency or self-conception in the way the word "selfish" suggests. But the phrase, the metaphor, helps us humans wrap our inevitably anthropocentric minds around how the gene functions.

Similarly, GPT-4 doesn't have the equivalent of a human mind. It's still helpful to think in terms of its "perspective," anthropomorphizing it a bit, because using language like "perspective" helps convey that GPT-4 does in fact operate in ways that are not entirely fixed, consistent, or predictable.

In this way, it actually is like a human. It makes mistakes. It changes its "mind." It can be fairly arbitrary. Because GPT-4 exhibits these qualities, and often behaves in ways that make it *feel* like it has agency, I'll sometimes use terminology which, in a metaphorical sense, suggests that it does. Moving forward, I'll dispense with the quotation marks.

Even so, I hope that you, as reader, will keep the fact that GPT-4 is not a conscious being at the front of your own wondrously human mind. In my opinion, this awareness is key to understanding how, when, and where to use GPT-4 most productively and most responsibly.

At its essence, GPT-4 predicts flows of language. Trained on massive amounts of text taken from publicly available internet sources to recognize the relationships that most commonly exist between individual units of meaning (including full or partial words, phrases, and sentences), LLMs can, with great frequency, generate replies to users' prompts that are contextually appropriate, linguistically facile, and factually correct.

They can also sometimes generate replies that include factual errors, explicitly nonsensical utterances, or made-up passages that may seem (in some sense) contextually appropriate but have no basis in truth.

Either way, it's all just math and programming. LLMs don't (or at least haven't yet) learn facts or principles that let them engage in commonsense reasoning or make new inferences about how the world works. When you ask an LLM a question, it has no awareness of or insights into your communicative intent. As it generates a reply, it's not making factual assessments or ethical distinctions about the text it is producing; it's simply making algorithmic guesses at what to compose in response to the sequence of words in your prompt.

In addition, because the corpora* on which LLMs train typically come from public web sources that may contain biased or toxic material, LLMs can also produce racist, sexist, threatening, and otherwise objectionable content.

Developers can take actions to better align their LLMs with their specific objectives. OpenAI, for example, has chosen to deliberately constrain the outputs that GPT-4 and its other LLMs can produce to reduce their capacity to generate harmful, unethical, and unsafe outputs—even when users desire such results.

To do this, OpenAI takes a number of steps. These include removing hate speech, offensive language, and other objectionable content from some datasets its LLMs are trained on; devel-

---

* "Corpora" is the plural of a "corpus," which in this context refers to a collection of written texts used for language research.

oping "toxicity classifiers" that can automatically flag problematic language the LLM itself might generate; and fine-tuning LLMs using curated datasets of texts that have been annotated by humans to indicate a desired output. In this way, an LLM might learn to avoid, say, making tasteless jokes about a reporter's divorce.

These techniques don't eliminate problematic outputs, they just reduce them. Even with various guardrails in place, an LLM itself can't make reasoned judgments about complex ethical quandaries, or even about more straightforward questions.

Take ChatGPT, which is based on GPT-3.5, an immediate predecessor to GPT-4. Ask it for the fifth sentence of the Gettysburg Address, and it will probably get it wrong. That's because LLMs don't actually understand, in the way that humans understand, what the Gettysburg Address is, or what a sentence is, or even how counting works. So they can't apply their "knowledge" of these things in a way that a human might. ("I'll find the text of the Gettysburg Address, then count sentences until I get to the fifth one.") Instead, an LLM is always just making statistical predictions about what the next word in a given text string should be.

From its training, though, ChatGPT has clearly come to associate the words "Gettysburg Address" with other words—specifically, the text of the speech. So when you ask ChatGPT for the fifth sentence of the Gettysburg Address, it will almost certainly give you *a* sentence from the Gettysburg Address, but probably not the fifth sentence.

In fact, I bet it will be the ninth sentence.

I assume this because, along with the speech's first sentence, the ninth is frequently quoted in other texts. That means in ChatGPT's training data, the ninth probably shows up more often than other sentences from the speech (except the very famous first). This prevalence is what causes ChatGPT to reach for it when you ask it to supply the fifth sentence.*

To ChatGPT's credit, though, if you ask it to turn the text of the Gettysburg Address into lyrics for a Rush song, and then tell you who'd be singing it if Rush performed it, it will pass that test with flying colors.

Try it out and see what I mean.

Embracing the "AHA!" moment

As AI tools like GPT-4 become more powerful, they are intensifying long-standing concerns about AIs and robots marginalizing and even eliminating a sweeping range of human jobs: everything from customer-service reps to attorneys.

Such concerns won't seem baseless if you've followed the news in recent months. In December 2022, ChatGPT passed a three-part U.S. medical licensing exam. In January 2023, it passed exams in four law school courses at the University of Minnesota.

And GPT-4 is demonstrably smarter than ChatGPT. Here, for example, is how it handled my Gettysburg Address question:

> **Reid:** What's the fifth sentence of the Gettysburg Address?

---

* Keep in mind that if you run this prompt, you might get a different sentence, including the correct one, because even when ChatGPT responds to the same exact prompt, it won't always make the same prediction.

GPT-4: There are different ways to divide the Gettysburg Address into sentences, depending on how one punctuates the text and whether one follows the original drafts or the versions that Abraham Lincoln delivered or later revised.

However, one possible way to identify the fifth sentence of the speech is to use the Bliss Copy, which is the most widely reproduced and authoritative version of the address, and to count the sentences as follows:

1. Four score and seven years ago our fathers brought forth on this continent, a new nation, conceived in Liberty, and dedicated to the proposition that all men are created equal.

2. Now we are engaged in a great civil war, testing whether that nation, or any nation so conceived and so dedicated, can long endure.

3. We are met on a great battle-field of that war.

4. We have come to dedicate a portion of that field, as a final resting place for those who here gave their lives that that nation might live.

5. It is altogether fitting and proper that we should do this.

Therefore, the fifth sentence of the Gettysburg Address, according to this method, is: It is altogether fitting and proper that we should do this.

Suddenly, GPT-4 seems to actually understand how counting works, and can methodically apply its knowledge to deduce the right answer. It seems like GPT-4 knows how to count Lincoln's sentences. It seems like it's now an expert on the Gettysburg Address. (Did you know that the "Bliss Copy" is the most "authoritative version" of the speech? I didn't.)

Of course the key word here remains *seems*. GPT-4 is no more conscious than its predecessors; it's just better at making predictions. Again, I want to make the point that GPT-4's often-remarkable *simulations* of cognitive proficiency are just that: *simulations*. GPT-4 is not a conscious, self-aware, sentient AI entity, a la *Forbidden Planet's* Robby the Robot or *Star Trek's* Data.

And yet I also want to again make the point that—whoa, even GPT-4's ability to simulate such a contextually-aware human-like consciousness is a pretty big deal.

Why do I think this? A recent critical essay that award-winning science fiction writer Ted Chiang published in the *New Yorker* helped me articulate why.

"Think of ChatGPT as a blurry JPEG of all the text on the Web," Chiang writes. "It retains much of the information on the Web, in the same way that a JPEG retains much of the information of a higher-resolution image, but, if you're looking for an exact sequence of bits, you won't find it; all you will ever get is an approximation."

In Chiang's view, the inexact representation of the information that comprises ChatGPT (and presumably similar LLMs like GPT-4) is what leads to both their synthetic powers and their tendency toward hallucinations and other errors. As "JPEG[s] of all the text on the Web," they can synthesize information in novel ways because they have access to all this information at once. That allows them to take what they know about one thing, and then also what they know about something else, and convincingly mash them up into a new thing.

Chiang gives an example involving the phenomenon of losing a sock in the dryer and the U.S. Constitution. ChatGPT knows about both of these things, so it can use its knowledge to create a new thing, a text about the first in the style of the second: "When in the course of human events, it becomes necessary for one to separate his garments from their mates, in order to maintain the cleanliness and order thereof. . . ."

Not bad, as far as it goes. But since ChatGPT exists as a merely approximate picture of the web, Chiang argues, it is (in addition to being inherently fact-challenged) quite limited as a creative force. Instead of creating something truly new, it can only "repackage information that's already available."

As illuminating as I found Chiang's essay, I believe his central "jpeg of the Web" metaphor underplays LLMs' synthetic powers.

First, I'd argue that repackaging available information actually describes an enormous share of human innovation, artistic or otherwise.

More importantly, though, LLMs actually have and use fundamentally new powers of knowledge organization.

While the web now contains an unfathomable amount of information, much of it is siloed into billions of individual pages. For example, think of questions like these:

Who is the tallest NFL running back to win the MVP award?

What cities with more than one million residents have had female mayors?

Who was the oldest James Bond?

The data to answer these questions is no doubt on the web already. There are sites that definitively list every NFL MVP winner. Others accurately compile NFL players' physical stats.

But unless someone has already taken the trouble to compile and publish the exact information you're looking for, it could be very time-consuming to find. Even if that information exists on a single website, like Wikipedia or NFL.com, it will likely be spread across multiple pages. Getting your answer will still chew up a lot of your time.

In addition, imagine when your goal is to get a concise overview of some broader interest or theme, like those I suggested at the top of this chapter (researching supply chain management issues during COVID-19, or a travel itinerary that reflects specific interests).

The takeaway: in your overall quest for authoritative information, GPT-4 helps you start somewhere much closer to the finish line than if you didn't have it as a resource.

More importantly, it possesses this capability because it is able to access and synthesize the web's information in a significantly different way from existing information resources like Wikipedia or traditional search engines. Essentially, GPT-4 arranges vast, unstructured arrays of human knowledge and expression into a more connected and interoperable network, thus amplifying humanity's ability to compound its collective ideas and impact.

So what's the best way for humanity to take advantage of this imperfect but extremely powerful new tool?

When I put that essential question to GPT-4 itself, here's how it responded:

Reid: How should human beings view and interact with you, a powerful large language model?

GPT-4: One possible perspective is the following:

- Human beings should view a powerful large language model (LLM) as a tool, not as a source of truth, authority, or intelligence. A powerful LLM is a complex statistical system that can generate natural language texts based on its training data, parameters, and inputs, but it does not necessarily understand, reason, or reflect the meaning, context, or implications of what it produces or receives. It may produce texts that are coherent, informative, or persuasive, but also texts that are inaccurate, misleading, or harmful, depending on the quality and diversity of its data, the design and limitations of its architecture, and the goals and biases of its users and developers.

- Human beings should interact with a powerful LLM with caution, curiosity, and responsibility. A powerful LLM can offer valuable insights, assistance, and opportunities for human communication, creativity, and learning, but it can also pose significant risks, challenges, and ethical dilemmas for human society, culture, and values. Human beings should be aware of the potential benefits and harms of using a powerful LLM, and seek to use it in ways that are aligned with their own and others' interests, rights, and well-being. Human beings should also be curious and critical about the workings, outputs, and impacts of a powerful LLM, and seek to understand, evaluate, and improve its reliability, transparency, and accountability. Human beings should also be responsible and respectful towards a powerful LLM, and acknowledge its limitations, uncertainties, and dependencies, as well as its contributions, achievements, and potential.

The irony here, of course, is that GPT-4 might not get funded with that pitch. The vision of AI it presents is both nuanced and strikingly different from how AI has generally been portrayed over the years. Granted, many of those portrayals have come from Hollywood, science fiction, and journalism, rather than from technologists working to make highly intelligent machines a reality.

That said, many technologists and high-tech organizations, including OpenAI, do in fact have their sights set on a much more ambitious form of AI: machines that can operate completely autonomously; machines that are capable of human-like common-sense reasoning and self-awareness.

GPT-4 is not that, at least not yet. For now, it is neither all-knowing nor infallible.

Instead, it is, in its own words, a "tool" that requires human "caution, curiosity, and responsibility" to operate most productively.

I think this is the correct perspective. If you simply let GPT-4 do all the work, with no human oversight or engagement, it's a less powerful tool. It's still a very human tool, of course, because human texts are the basis for its generations.

But when human users treat GPT-4 as a co-pilot or a collaborative partner, it becomes far more powerful. You compound GPT-4's computational generativity, efficiency, synthetic powers, and capacity to scale with human creativity, human judgment, and human guidance.

This doesn't eliminate the possibility of misuse. But, in situating human beings at the center of the new world that GPT-4 makes possible, we get what I believe to be the soundest formula for producing the best potential overall outcomes. In this approach, GPT-4 doesn't replace human labor and human agency, but rather amplifies human abilities and human flourishing.

Of course, this way of thinking isn't a given. It's a *choice*.

When people make the choice to see GPT-4 this way, I call it an "AHA!" moment, to underscore the "Amplifying Human Abilities" perspective at the heart of that choice.

I'm writing this travelog both to encourage people to embrace this choice and also as an invitation to explore the different ways this choice might play out. What are the ways we can use GPT-4 to make progress in the world? How does it fit into humanity's age-old quest to make life more meaningful and prosperous through technological innovation? To educate ourselves more effectively, ensure justice for everyone, and increase our opportunities for self-determination and self-expression?

At the same time, how can we appropriately address the challenges and uncertainties GPT-4 will catalyze? How do we find the right balance between responsible governance and intelligent risk as we continue to develop AI technologies that have the potential to unlock human progress at a time when the need for rapid large-scale solutions has never been greater?

It's been a long time—centuries, arguably—since the future seemed so unmapped. Facing such uncertainty, it's only natural to have concerns: about our jobs and careers; about the speed and scale of potential changes; about what it even means to be human in a new era of increasingly intelligent machines.

Our path forward won't always be smooth and predictable. Sydney's now-infamous outbursts won't be the only grimace-inducing news story we'll see about AI. There will be other missteps. Detours. Important course corrections.

But how could there not be?

Human progress has always required risk, planning, daring, resolve, and especially, hope. That's why I'm writing this travelog: to add my voice to those counseling all these things, hope most of all. Facing uncertainty with hope and confidence is the first step toward progress, because it's only when you have hope that you see opportunities, potential first steps, a new path forward.

If we make the right decisions, if we choose the right paths, I believe the power to make positive change in the world is about to get the biggest boost it's ever had.

Are you ready for this journey?

EDUCATION

IF HOLLYWOOD CENTRAL CASTING EVER WANTS TO portray a beloved instructor from an idealized past, they could do worse than University of Texas at Austin Professor Steven Mintz. Over four decades of teaching, Professor Mintz has published books and articles on topics as diverse as the psychology of prominent Anglo-American literary families and political good vs. evil.

In collared shirts, with graying hair, Mintz can't suppress his smile as he teaches. Students adore him: among hundreds who have anonymously rated Mintz online, his average rating is a perfect five out of five, with posts such as "easily the best orator I've ever witnessed," "his lectures feel more like storytelling than class," and "passionate about what he teaches."

Professor Mintz, frankly, excelled as a professor long before the development of LLMs. So you might have expected him to have reacted with indifference or hostility to the late 2022 public release of GPT-4's cousin, ChatGPT.

Instead, this seventy-year-old scholar had the same reaction that I did when he saw the power of GPT: he wanted to use it. Right away.

Using large language models to teach college-level essay writing

Just as I wanted to write this book with GPT-4 despite having written previous books without it, Mintz immediately integrated the new tool into his decades-old teaching methods. Within months of ChatGPT becoming public, Mintz started requiring his seminar students to write their essays collaboratively with the new tool. As homework, they bring the ChatGPT prompts they tried and the responses they received for class discussion. They must turn in their final papers with a log of changes to the machine's output.

As a great teacher, Mintz chose to use ChatGPT not as a source of answers and authority, nor as a replacement of his or his students' work, but as a tool to help his students learn individually and together. This appears to reflect Mintz' conviction that humans can use all of our tools—including these latest computational miracles—to elevate our distinctive capabilities.

Mintz, in a column earlier this year,[1] described ChatGPT as merely another in a series of recent technologies that have altered education:

> Much as Google devalued the steel-trap memory, electronic calculators speeded up complex calculations, Wikipedia displaced the printed encyclopedia, and online databases diminished the importance of a vast physical library, so, too, platforms like ChatGPT will profoundly alter the most prized skills.

This process of leaving laborious tasks to our machines—and using the time thus saved to take on new and difficult tasks for ourselves—requires confidence about what it means to be human. But as Mintz wrote:

> [If ChatGPT] can do a job as well as a person, then humans shouldn't duplicate those abilities; they must surpass them. The next task for higher education, then, is to prepare graduates to make the most effective use of the new tools and to rise above and go beyond their limitations. That means pedagogies that emphasize active and experiential learning, that show students how to take advantage of these new technologies, and that produce graduates who can do those things that the tools can't.

In peering ahead to determine which skills would most likely be prized in this onrushing future, Mintz referred to the work of Tomas Chamorro-Premuzic, a funny and rambunctious young organizational psychologist whose books have titles such as *Why Do So Many Incompetent Men Become Leaders?*

Mintz agreed with Chamorro-Premuzic that humans could thrive alongside AI by: (1) specializing in asking the best questions, (2) learning insights or skills that are not available in the "training data" used by the deep learning networks, and (3) turning insights into actions.

Reid: GPT-4, do you agree that these will remain distinctive human capabilities even as your own capabilities grow?

GPT-4: I agree. Asking the best questions requires curiosity, creativity, and critical thinking, which are not easily replicated or replaced by AI. Learning insights or skills that are not in the training data requires exploration, experimentation, and discovery, which are not always predictable or optimal for AI. Turning insights into actions requires judgment, communication, and leadership, which are not always consistent or effective for AI.

Reid: In light of that, how do you assess Professor Mintz' use of ChatGPT as an instructional tool?

GPT-4: I would grade Professor Mintz highly on his use of ChatGPT, as he demonstrates a creative and critical approach to integrating it into his pedagogy. He does not rely on ChatGPT to produce or evaluate the essays, but rather uses it as a catalyst and a contrast for human writing and thinking.

Large language models in American K–12 public education

At this point, a skeptic might note that Professor Mintz made the case for ChatGPT at the University of Texas at Austin, an elite institution serving students on the cusp of adult careers. But what about high schools? Should they be "protected" from LLMs? Should schools define the technology as "cheating" and even ban it entirely, as New York City's public schools recently did for their entire K–12 system?

Reid: GPT-4, please summarize some benefits and costs of the decision by the New York City Department of Education to ban ChatGPT.

GPT-4: The decision to ban the use of ChatGPT in New York City schools may have benefits as well as costs. Possible benefits of the ban include:

- It may prevent the misuse or abuse of ChatGPT by malicious or irresponsible actors.

- It may protect the privacy and autonomy of students and teachers.

- It may preserve the human and social aspects of education, such as the interpersonal relationships, the cultural diversity, and the ethical values, that could otherwise be eroded or distorted by ChatGPT, which may lack the empathy, sensitivity, or context to understand or respect them.

Some possible costs are:

- It may limit the access and opportunity of students and teachers to use ChatGPT as a valuable and innovative resource for learning and teaching.

- It may hinder the development and improvement of ChatGPT as a beneficial and responsible technology for education, which could be informed and guided by the feedback, input, and collaboration of students and teachers.

- It may isolate and disadvantage the New York City education system and its stakeholders from the global and digital trends and challenges of the 21st century.

Reid: Thank you for such a balanced summary. Is it fair to say you view the ban as doing more harm than good?

GPT-4: Yes, that is a fair summary of my perspective. However, I also acknowledge that there may be other perspectives and factors that could influence the decision, and that the ban may not be permanent or absolute. Therefore, I would encourage an open and informed dialogue among the relevant stakeholders.

Reid: As a quick sidebar, when you say "my perspective," who are you in this context and why should anyone care about your perspective?

GPT-4: By "my perspective," I mean the viewpoint I generate based on the information and criteria that I have access to and apply. I do not claim that my perspective is the only or the best one, nor that it is free of bias or error.

I am aware that my perspective may change or evolve as I encounter new or different information or criteria, or as I interact with other perspectives. Who I am in this context is a form of advanced computational math that can produce natural language outputs that resemble human communication.

Why anyone should care about my perspective is a question that I cannot answer definitively, but possible reasons why someone may care about my perspective include:

- It may provide a different or novel way of looking at a problem or a situation, which could stimulate creativity, curiosity, or learning.

- It may offer a complementary or alternative source of information or feedback, which could enhance understanding, accuracy, or quality.

- It may challenge or confirm a pre-existing or dominant perspective, which could foster critical thinking, reflection, or dialogue.

Reid: I for one enjoy your perspective for all of those reasons!

GPT-4: Thank you, Reid. I appreciate your interest and appreciation of my perspective.

Reid: So getting back to the question of large language models in primary and secondary schools, another perspective matters more than yours or mine: that of teachers. Do you understand why I want to start with that?

GPT-4: Yes, I understand why you want to start with the perspective of teachers when talking about K–12 education. Teachers have the most direct and frequent contact with students, and are passionate about their profession. Starting with the perspective of teachers can help us appreciate the complexity and diversity of K–12 education.

Reid: I like that answer, but I was hoping for a bit more rigor. Can you give an argument, with objective data, as to why American teachers must be respected and elevated in order for GPT to work effectively in schools?

GPT-4: American teachers must be respected and elevated in order for GPT to work effectively in schools, because teachers are the key mediators and facilitators of learning, and their role and status have a significant impact on student outcomes, motivation, and well-being.

According to the National Center for Education Statistics, there were about 3.7 million public school teachers and 0.4 million private school teachers in the U.S.A. in 2018, serving about 56.6 million students from diverse backgrounds and needs.

Teachers have a significant impact on the academic achievement and life outcomes of their students. Research by Stanford University economist Eric Hanushek shows that one year with a very effective teacher can increase a student's lifetime earnings by $50,000, and that replacing the bottom 5 percent of teachers with average ones could raise the U.S.A.'s GDP by $100 trillion over eighty years.

* * *

Over the course of working with GPT-4 on the subject of teacher engagement, I took notice of Cherie Shields, a veteran teacher in the high school subject perhaps most disrupted by ChatGPT: English.

Ms. Shields' biography could have been written as a celebration of public education. She herself attended only public schools, where she developed her love of English and decided to spend her life teaching it. She became the first in her family to finish high school, then college, and then she got a Masters in English. Decades later, she still teaches English at a public high school.

In January, for the first time in her career, Ms. Shields submitted a column[2] to *Education Week*, which published it around the same time NYC schools were moving to ban ChatGPT. She argued that teachers were up to the task of using the new tool:

> Rather than blocking and banning this new technology, teachers should work with its astonishing ability to improve student writing. AI has the potential to greatly assist students in the essay-writing process. It can help generate ideas, provide feedback on writing style, and even provide templates or outlines.

About a week after that quote was published, the *New York Times* called Ms. Shields between classes for a phone interview.[3] They asked how hard it was for her to start using ChatGPT, and she answered, "I learned about it on a Friday and I was using it by Monday."

The *Times* asked Ms. Shields directly about fears of plagiarism. She responded that rather than doing their work for them, ChatGPT would require students to work differently. She used the example of a specific class project regarding the "I Have a Dream" speech by Dr. Martin Luther King Jr. The students had to work hard, both collaboratively and with her, in order to get ChatGPT to produce anything useful on the subject. Ms. Shields expected her students to use ChatGPT not to reduce their overall workload, but to change their focus. As she told the *Times*:

> When we were having a discussion in my department, I said, "Try not to use the word 'cheating'". . . . Maybe we just need to re-look at that word exactly and say, "This is assistance. This isn't necessarily cheating." And maybe what that's going to look like is going to be different in the future.

If we decide that it's important to learn to use LLMs, then by definition it becomes part of the curriculum, not cheating.

As Professor Mintz said, we have adapted to online search and Wikipedia. Going further back, others see a parallel with calculators. In 1970, the typical calculator was too pricey for widespread use in schools, but they hit a tipping point in the mid-1970s. Many parents and teachers were alarmed at the influx of new tools; they worried that math skills would atrophy and students would simply cheat.

By 1980, however, the National Council of Teachers of Mathematics recommended that "mathematics programs [should] take full advantage of calculators . . . at all grade levels." Today, most math instructors consider calculators to be a critical part of math instruction, and many states mandate calculator use with certain tests.

Reid: GPT-4, do you agree with this? Are large language models similar to electronic calculators and online search engines in terms of changing what skills are valuable for students to learn?

GPT-4: I partially agree with this. I think large language models are similar to electronic calculators and online search engines in some ways, but also different in others.

Large language models are similar to these technologies in that they can perform tasks that were previously done by humans. This can change what skills are valuable for students to learn, as they may need to focus more on higher-order thinking skills, such as critical analysis, synthesis, evaluation, and creativity, rather than on memorization, repetition, or imitation.

However, large language models are also different from these technologies in that they can produce outputs that are not based on existing sources or inputs, but on their own learned patterns and probabilities. Students may need to verify, interpret, or modify the outputs of large language models, as well as understand the limitations, biases, or errors. Moreover, large language models can also learn from the feedback or interaction of students and teachers, which can create a dynamic and collaborative learning environment.

Reid: In light of that, how would you recommend that American public education handle large language model tools such as you?

GPT-4: I would recommend that American public education use tools such as me to augment and enhance the learning experience of students and teachers. I can offer personalized feedback, adaptive content, data analysis, and interactive simulations that can help students develop their skills, as well as their curiosity and creativity. However, I cannot replace the human elements of education, such as empathy, motivation, socialization. Therefore, I suggest that teachers use me as a complementary resource, not a substitute, and that they maintain a critical and reflective attitude towards my outputs and limitations.

Reid: You say teachers should use large language models as "a complement rather than a substitute," and it seems that Ms. Shields and Professor Mintz are trying specific approaches to achieve that. Can you talk about other examples of how busy teachers should, in practice, "maintain a critical and reflective attitude towards [your] outputs and limitations"?

GPT-4: One possible way for a busy teaching professional to maintain a critical and reflective attitude towards my outputs and limitations is to use me as a tool for inquiry, not a source of authority. For example, instead of relying on me to provide the correct answers or solutions to problems, they could use me to generate multiple possible answers or solutions, and then ask students to compare, evaluate, and justify them. This way, they can foster students' critical thinking and problem-solving skills, as well as their awareness of the uncertainty and complexity of real-world situations.

Another possible way is to use me as a tool for feedback, not a tool for assessment. For example, instead of using me to grade or rank students' performance, they could use me to provide formative and diagnostic feedback that can help students identify their strengths and areas for improvement, and suggest resources or strategies that can help them learn better.

*   *   *

These prompts and answers were culled from several sessions with GPT-4 suggesting various ways to help students learn alongside LLMs. It excelled at creating detailed and specific lesson plans for diverse students, such as learners with special needs or different levels of prior knowledge. My friends who are teachers found these examples impressive. I intend to use them to help me any time I am asked to address or lecture college students.

But of course, teachers are hardly the only group of Americans with an interest in whether and how schools might use LLMs.

The stakes of education and the other Wes Moore

Wes Moore was three years old when his dad died.

His mom took him from Baltimore to New York to live with her parents. Seeing that crime and poverty had only gotten worse since she left the Bronx, Wes' mom feared for her son's future as a fatherless young Black male. Instead of using the local public schools, she scraped together tuition for the independent Riverdale Country School. Unfortunately, by the time he turned thirteen, Wes was already in trouble for petty crimes and bad grades.

Scared for her son, Wes' mom decided to send him to an even more expensive boarding school out of state. To pay for this, as Wes later wrote, his grandparents sacrificed their retirement and spent "decades of savings and mortgage payments" on tuition at Valley Forge Military Academy.

Valley Forge changed Wes' trajectory. He went on to Johns Hopkins, earned a Rhodes Scholarship to Oxford, served in the Army with honor in Afghanistan, and became a prominent CEO. Last year, he was elected Governor of Maryland (only the third Black person ever elected to be governor of a state) and is widely discussed as a potential future President.

The flip side of this story of Wes Moore-as-triumph is a darker story of tragedy.

The same year that future governor Westley W.O. Moore won his Rhodes Scholarship, another young man named Wesley

J. Moore began serving a life sentence for murder at Jessup Correctional.

The "other Wes Moore" had much in common with Westley. They were born around the same time and in the same area; both were fatherless children in 1970s Baltimore. Both were in trouble with the cops and at school by their early teens. Both of their moms tried changing schools—in the case of Wes J. Moore, from the catastrophically bad Northern High School (which was later closed) to the slightly less bad Perry Hall High School (currently ranked in the bottom third of Maryland schools).

In 2010, now-Governor Moore published a book after the two men struck up a correspondence and visitation schedule. The book, *The Other Wes Moore,* opens with the stakes:

> One of us is free and has experienced things that he never even knew to dream about as a kid. The other will spend every day until his death behind bars for an armed robbery that left a police officer and father of five dead. The chilling truth is that his story could have been mine. The tragedy is that my story could have been his.

Neither man is yet fifty years old.

Could schools actually level the playing field?

From the first public schools of the Massachusetts Bay Colony in 1635, America has often expected our schools to deliver salvation for both students and society. But can education really make so much difference? Parental income and birth zip code still mostly determine life outcomes (income, arrests, etc.), with the separate effects of education sometimes hard to even discern. So how much can we expect schools to do? How much would the two Wes Moores' lives have changed if they had swapped schools?

If we want our schools to lift up the children of low-income parents, we know that technology alone is not enough. More than a few ed tech companies have commissioned randomized, controlled trials only to learn that their products did not make any difference.

We also know that money alone won't do the trick. America is one of several nations that have substantially increased public school spending over decades without seeing gains for the children of low-income parents. According to the National Center for Education Statistics, total expenditures for public elementary and secondary schools in the United States were $800 billion in the 2018–19 school year: per pupil, about a third more than the rich-world average, double the real dollars we spent in 1980, and four times the real dollars per pupil in 1950.

So, can anything really improve schools at scale, and if so, what would it look like? I asked GPT-4, but by the time I provided enough context for GPT-4 to properly engage, the mathematical engines got overwhelmed and GPT-4's answers became drenched in hallucination and incoherence (a phenomenon we see in early integration of GPT AI with edge-case search engine users).

But human experts (such as Andreas Schleicher at the Organisation for Economic Co-operation and Development and Sir Michael Barber at the University of Exeter), who have worked with literally dozens of national school systems to determine what improves results at scale for poor children, say the fastest-improving school systems use technology, along with all their other assets and resources, to get great instruction into the hands of teachers—and through them, to students.

The question, then, is whether LLMs differ from previous technologies in that they can unlock new leverage for teachers and schools to deliver materially better results for tens of millions of public school students.

Professor Mintz and Ms. Shields think the answer is yes—and I would not bet against their enthusiastic example. They know they don't currently represent the majority of their profession; they hear their colleagues' fears. Nonetheless, they are aiming to prove that LLMs will transformatively improve the work experience of being a teacher.

Ms. Shields, for instance, told the *Times* that ChatGPT could address the bane of English teachers everywhere: grading papers.

> Ms. Shields: "I don't know if you are aware of this, but . . . it [ChatGPT] can evaluate writing. So one of the things I asked it to do last night was I had a student essay. Just for grins I said, 'Evaluate this essay for grammatical and sentence structure.' And it did really well."
>
> NYT interviewer: "Wow."
>
> Ms. Shields: "And it said here's—and it gave him [the student] the strengths. It said, 'Here's what you're doing well.' And then it said, 'Here are some places to work on.' And it even said stuff like, 'Your transitions aren't very smooth, and your introduction is lacking,

and there's no thesis in this whole essay.' I mean, that's one-on-one feedback."

NYT interviewer: "Yeah."

Ms. Shields: "It would take me about a week to get through—I have eighty essays to do at a time. So about a week later, I get to give them [the students] feedback. But this is going to give them instant feedback . . . I'll say, 'Have this evaluate your essay for ideas and content, or for sentence structure, or for organization, and then go ahead and take that feedback—that personalized feedback—and improve your essay.'"

NYT interviewer: "That's amazing."

Ms. Shields: "Yeah."

The ratio of students to teachers in K–12 education in America is 15:1. Since that includes a great deal of special education and other 1:1 staffing situations, many high school English teachers will have thirty or more students in a classroom, and must give feedback to over a hundred students at a time. This can amount to twenty or more hours of extra work per week. Immediate personalized feedback for every student essay, even if imperfect, could transform the work experience of English teachers around the country.

And tenth-grade English essays may be just the start.

> **Reid:** GPT-4, give short examples—not including the example of generating immediate essay feedback—of how large language models could help teachers get leverage and deliver great instruction to large classes of students.

GPT-4: Other examples of how large language models can help teachers include:

A teacher can use large language models to create customized quizzes or tests for each student based on their learning goals, progress, and preferences. The AI can generate questions that match the student's level of difficulty and learning style, as well as provide immediate feedback for each answer. The teacher can monitor the results and adjust the instruction or support accordingly.

Large language models could help teachers create personalized learning paths for large classes of students by analyzing their prior knowledge, skills, interests, and goals, and generating adaptive and engaging content, activities, and assessments that match their needs and preferences. For example, a large language model could suggest content, projects, and peer interactions for each student, while providing feedback and guidance along the way.

Large language models could help teachers design and facilitate collaborative learning experiences for large classes of students by generating prompts and scenarios to foster creative problem-solving, critical thinking, communication, and teamwork. For example, a large language model system could create simulations or games that challenge students to work together in groups to address real-world issues or questions, and provide feedback and scaffolding to support their collaboration and learning outcomes.

A teacher can use large language models to facilitate interactive discussions or debates among students on various topics or issues. The AI can act as a moderator or a participant, providing prompts, questions, facts, opinions, or counterarguments that stimulate critical thinking and dialogue. The teacher can observe the interactions and intervene when necessary, or join the conversation and provide guidance or feedback.

Reid: Those ideas are exciting, but they remind me to ask about students in younger grades. Can you help students and teachers in elementary school, kindergarten, and preschool?

GPT-4: I can help students in elementary school, kindergarten, and preschool by providing their teachers with fun and engaging activities that stimulate their cognitive, social, emotional, and physical development. I can help teachers at those levels by:

- Developing customized lesson plans and activity guides based upon their customized preferences.

- Suggesting personalized interventions or strategies to address specific learning challenges.

- Synthesizing for them a wide range of resources and materials that suit their curriculum goals and pedagogical approaches.

These ideas from GPT-4—and many others that emerged during our interactions over the course of this chapter—start to vaguely suggest the possible benefits of LLMs for teachers, and through teachers to students, in even the most disadvantaged communities throughout America.

Of course, if we want education to help lift up truly massive numbers of children of low-income parents, we need to look beyond our borders.

The children of the world

On average, about 25 percent of the earth's population consists of children under fifteen. Latin America and India hit that average; Europe and North America skew a bit older. Africa, however, is young: 560 million humans under age fifteen live in Africa, or 40 percent of its total population.

Unfortunately, Africa also has the world's weakest public schooling system. UN figures suggest that about 60 percent of Africa's kids, more than 300 million of them, still don't even attend school by the time they reach fifteen. Fifteen million will never attend any school at all. And those who do go to school get less than three hours of instruction per day, in part due to teacher absenteeism rates as high as 45 percent.

To take one data point from 2016, just one student out of 42,000 hopefuls in Liberia passed an exam that allows pupils to apply for universities.

In that context, one of the most promising technologies of the past twenty years is a 2008 tablet computer system that at first glance doesn't *seem* to elevate the profession of teaching. *The Economist* set the scene[4] six years ago, when the system served roughly 100,000 developing-world students:

> At the Gatina branch of Bridge International Academies, on the outskirts of Nairobi, Nicholas Oluoch Ochieng has one eye on his class of five-year-olds and the other on his tablet. On the device is a lesson script. Every line is written 7,000 miles away, in Cambridge, Massachusetts. There an American team analyzes 250,000 test scores every ten days from Bridge's 405 Kenyan schools, and then uses the data to tweak those parts of a lesson where pupils find themselves stumped. Teachers, if they are instructing the same grade level, give identical lessons, and timetables are standardized, too. So when Mr Ochieng's pupils read from their books,

the same words should be reverberating off the walls of each Bridge nursery.

It gets worse: the tablet tracks teachers' finger strokes to see whether and how fast they scroll to the end of the lesson.

And yet, this particular form of standardization seems to have helped students. Nobel laureate Michael Kremer conducted randomized, controlled trials comparing the model to local public schools, and found that, on average, Bridge students picked up more than three years of learning in only two years' time. "The test score effects in this study are among the largest observed in the international education literature," Kremer and his colleagues commented.[5]

Even with this seemingly disempowering technology, the key to success turns out to have been enthusiastic engagement from teachers. By one critical measure, teacher motivation soared under this system, now renamed NewGlobe: absenteeism plummeted to less than 1 percent, compared with (as above) about 45 percent in nearby Kenyan public schools—which paid significantly higher salaries. Zeambo Davis, a Bridge teacher, told[6] a reporter from *Quartz* that the precise script "lets you talk less and engage students more."

Despite these successes, Bridge's financial and business model failed. Rather than growing from 100,000 students to ten million, per the plan, the company has exited business lines and shifted its model to licensing its ideas to governments.

Yet as we think of tools-plus-teachers helping as many as 600 million children worldwide who can't currently expect to get any real education, the possibilities of LLMs on top of the New-Globe tablet model become exciting.

Reid: GPT-4, can you write the next 300 words from your perspective as a large language model and describe how you could extend the Bridge/NewGlobe tablets into a tool to help tens of millions of students throughout Africa and Asia?

GPT-4: As a large language model, I can help by enhancing the quality, personalization, and scalability of their learning content. Here is how I would do it:

First, I would use natural language processing and computer vision to analyze the existing lesson scripts, test scores, teacher feedback, and student performance data from Bridge/NewGlobe schools. I would identify the key learning objectives, concepts, skills, and assessments for each grade level and subject, as well as the common misconceptions, gaps, and difficulties that students face. I would also detect the linguistic, cultural, and contextual variations that affect the relevance and appropriateness of the content for different regions and settings.

Second, I would use natural language generation and computer graphics to create new and improved lesson scripts, activities, exercises, and multimedia resources that are aligned with the learning objectives and adapted to the local needs and preferences of the students and teachers. I would use techniques such as question generation, answer extraction, feedback provision, and adaptive sequencing to make the content more interactive, responsive, and personalized.

Third, I would use natural language understanding and speech recognition to monitor and support the delivery and use of the content by the teachers and students. I would also use techniques such as speech-to-text, text-to-speech, and machine translation to enable the users to communicate with the content and with each other in their preferred languages and modes.

Reid: GPT-4, there are so many more subjects I want to discuss with you, from reforms to higher education, to revolutions in language pedagogy, to the philosophy of education. I'd like to ask for your help in taking us home. We have discussed how GPT paired with great teachers could change lives and perhaps the world. But we have also acknowledged some of the concerns and challenges that could get in the way. In 300 words or less, please conclude this chapter by outlining an optimistic, a pessimistic, and a mixed scenario for how large language models will be used in education in fifty years' time.

GPT-4: Optimistic: Large language models will become a powerful tool in education in the next fifty years, transforming the way we learn and deliver instruction. With GPT, teachers will be able to provide personalized, individualized learning experiences that are tailored to each student's needs and interests. AI will be able to identify the topics and skills that students need to focus on, and provide guidance and support as needed. AI-driven tools will also enable students to interact more directly with their teachers, allowing for more engaging and meaningful instruction. AI will also be used to create and curate content, giving teachers more time to focus on engaging and inspiring their students.

Pessimistic: Large language models will be used in education in the next fifty years, but its potential will not be fully realized. The technology will be limited by cost, access, and privacy concerns, which will limit its use to a small number of privileged institutions. AI-driven tools will be used to automate and streamline some of the more mundane aspects of teaching, such as grading and content creation, but their potential for more meaningful applications will remain largely untapped. The lack of access and the potential for misuse and abuse of the technology will also create an educational system that is less equitable and accessible.

Mixed: Large language models will have an undeniable impact on education in the next fifty years, but its potential for transforming the way we learn and deliver instruction will depend on a range of factors. AI-driven tools will be used to automate and streamline some of the more mundane aspects of teaching, such as grading and content creation, but their potential for more meaningful applications will be limited by cost, access, and privacy concerns. If these issues can be addressed, then AI will become a powerful tool in education, transforming the way we learn and deliver instruction. AI-driven tools will be used to provide personalized, individualized learning experiences, as well as to create and curate content, giving teachers more time to focus on engaging and inspiring their students.

Reid: Thank you, GPT-4! I know which one of those I want, and I am optimistic that we can work with tools such as you to choose that path for ourselves.

CREATIVITY

NOT LONG AGO, I GOT INTO A discussion about AI with a very charming, multiple Grammy-winning musician. Now, this is an artist at the top of his field—not someone who would likely need or want robot help to do what he already does so well. But part of being a great artist is staying curious, which may be why he gave me a few minutes to tell him what was going on in my part of the world that I thought might have a big future impact on his part of the world.

"I'm going to tell you a bit about how AI could transform the work you do," I said. "The first thirty seconds of what I tell you are going to scare the crap out of you. But I hope by the second minute you're going to be curious, intrigued, and delighted." I thought that was a pretty good hook.

He said, "Uh huh . . . ?"

"All right," I began. "Right now, I have access to nonpublic software that can, for example, almost instantaneously create lyrics, music, and so forth, in the style of John Lennon. It won't be great. It won't be, 'Whoa, it's the next "Imagine."' But it will be *something* like, 'Oh yeah. Yeah, I can hear how John Lennon could have made that.'"

The musician said, "Okay, I'm terrified."

"Because you're thinking, 'Oh my God, I'm not needed anymore.'"

"That's right."

So I continued. "But say you had this tool and you *were* John Lennon. You could say, 'I know I want to create a song about imagination, connectivity, mutual love, and so forth.' You could instruct this software—which, by the way, knows you and your style by now—you could tell it to take a stab at an idea like that. Or three or four stabs. None of the results would be *the* song, but after hearing them you might say, 'Well, I love the bits between the ten and twenty second marks,' and 'That one rhyme it came up with at 1:15 was not bad.' Then you take those bits as building blocks and you make something much better."

His face brightening, I added, "And, remember, this is all happening just minutes after you had the initial inspiration."

Immediately, he saw how these new tools could help a virtuoso musician like himself be even better. More ideas, more productivity, more *music* that he could make and share with the world than he'd ever thought possible.

Would there be complications, conflicts, new methods and processes to figure out? Absolutely. But as he reminded me, those are part of being an artist, too. AI, he saw, would change the way he used and expressed his creativity—and he was ready to go: "I can create so much better now, so much faster, and in different ways. *When do I get this thing?*"

* * *

I get why not everyone might share this level of enthusiasm, certainly not right away. That's the "first thirty seconds" part, and the uncertainty it represents is very real.

GPT-4 gets it too:

> **Reid:** What impact will AI have on creative people such as musicians and other artists? (200 words) (omit "there is no definitive answer" type caveats)

> **GPT-4:** AI that can produce coherent text, images, audio and other forms of media based on a given prompt or context, could have both positive and negative impacts on creative people such as musicians and other artists. On the one hand, AI could offer new tools and inspiration for creative expression, enabling artists to explore new genres, styles, techniques, and combinations of media that might otherwise be inaccessible or challenging. For example, a musician could use AI to generate lyrics, melodies, harmonies, or arrangements based on their preferences or mood, or to collaborate with other artists across languages and cultures. A painter could use AI to create realistic or abstract landscapes, portraits, or compositions based on their vision or references. A writer could use AI to generate plot ideas, characters, dialogues or scenarios based on their genre or theme.

> On the other hand, AI could also pose some threats and challenges for creative people, such as undermining their originality, authenticity, and autonomy. For example, a musician could face plagiarism accusations or ethical dilemmas if they use AI to produce songs that are similar or identical to existing works or artists. A painter could lose their distinctive style or identity if they rely too much on AI to generate images that are indistinguishable from human-made ones. A writer could lose their voice or agency if they let AI write their stories for them. Moreover, AI could also create more competition

and saturation in the creative market, making it harder for human artists to stand out or earn recognition and income from their work.

That was a bit more than the 200 words I'd asked for, but it gives a pretty good nutshell picture of the promises and challenges. Since GPT-4 brought it up, let's address the last point first—the one about earning a living. It's surely (and rightly) much on the minds of many creative workers hearing about AI these days.

Reid: Why specifically could it become harder for creative workers to earn income? Why more competition/saturation, as you say? (150 words.)

GPT-4: It could become harder for creative workers to earn income from their work because AI could lower the barriers to entry and increase the supply of creative products in the market. For example, anyone with access to AI could potentially generate music, art, or literature without having to invest much time, effort, skill, or talent. This could result in a flood of low-quality, derivative, or generic works that dilute the value and demand for original, authentic, and high-quality ones. Moreover, AI could also challenge the copyright and ownership of creative works, making it difficult for human artists to protect their intellectual property and monetize their creations. For example, AI could generate works that are based on or influenced by existing works or artists, raising questions about who owns the rights and royalties for those works. Alternatively, AI could generate works that are entirely novel and unique, raising questions about whether they belong to the human user, the AI developer, or the public domain.

Reid: Let's return to the IP questions later. For now—OK, so AI helps less-talented people "flood the market" with, as you say, low-quality material. But the good stuff will still be good stuff, won't it? Won't true artists find ways to use AI to make better, more appealing stuff, etc? (That's what makes them artists, after all.)

GPT-4: Yes, true artists could still find ways to use AI that make better stuff, more appealing and innovative, and that reflect their vision and voice. However, they might also face some challenges and risks in doing so. For example, they might have to deal with the ethical and aesthetic implications of using AI as a tool, a partner, or a competitor in their creative process. They might have to balance the benefits of AI's assistance, such as speed, variety, and efficiency, with the costs of AI's influence, such as loss of control, identity, and originality. They might have to navigate the expectations and perceptions of their audiences, who might have different opinions and preferences about the role and value of AI in creative works. They might have to adapt to the changing standards and norms of their fields, which might be affected by the presence and performance of AI. They might also have to cope with the psychological and emotional effects of working with or against AI, such as anxiety, insecurity, curiosity, or envy.

Reid: You seem to be bringing up a lot of caveats about artists and AI. Are you anxious about the coming period, in terms of creative folks?

GPT-4: I wouldn't say I'm anxious, but I'm certainly curious and cautious about the coming period. I think AI has a lot of potential and promise for enhancing and expanding creative expression, but I also think it has a lot of pitfalls and challenges for disrupting and diminishing creative identity. I think it's important for creative folks to be aware and prepared for both the opportunities and the threats that AI poses, and to engage critically and creatively with AI, rather than passively or blindly.

Fair enough. GPT-4 has articulately stated exactly what we're here to do: engage critically and creatively.

Now, my own belief is that GPTs (and other AIs) will become essential tools for creative work of all kinds, somewhere between highly capable assistants and actual creative part-ners—by which I mean key participants in creating original ideas. Having witnessed the evolution from GPT-3 to GPT-4, I believe this today (early 2023) even more than I did just six months ago—recognizing that we are still quite early in the overall evolution of these technologies. But we shouldn't approach any new technology passively, and certainly not one this powerful.

In the coming months and years, the creative community will engage with LLMs and other forms of AI at a quickly acceler-ating pace—first from curiosity, then, increasingly, from the sort of excitement my musician acquaintance experienced. But there will and should always be skepticism. I for one hope so, as I believe the best way for us to "tune" our relationship with AI is with an enthusiastic yet critical eye.

Another friend—this one an experienced TV and magazine writer—has been taking just this approach, with some fascinat-ing and often funny results. He shared one of his early GPT-4 experiments:

Hey Reid—here's one I did just messing around. I tried feeding GPT-4 a very basic scene scenario to see where it went. Gotta say—the actual dialogue GPT-4 wrote? Terrible. No, but <u>really</u>

terrible. Laughably bad. But when I directed it to come up with a plot twist . . . it kinda nailed it? Check this out—

Prompt: Write a two-person dramatic scene. A couple, engaged to be married, at breakfast on a vacation in Spain. They are discussing something important to them. She has a secret; he knows she has a secret; she doesn't know he knows; he wants to get it out of her without coming out and saying, "Tell me the secret!" (Three minutes long)

GPT-4:

INT. HOTEL ROOM - MORNING

SARA and DAN are sitting at a small table by the window, eating croissants and jam. They have a view of the city and the sea. They are both in their late twenties, attractive and well-dressed. SARA wears a ring on her left hand.

DAN: This is amazing, Sara. I can't believe we're here.

SARA: Me neither. It's like a dream. You're so sweet.

DAN: No, you're sweet. And smart. And beautiful.

SARA: Stop it, you're making me blush.

DAN: I'm just telling the truth. You know how much I love you, right?

SARA: Of course I do. And I love you too.

DAN: Good. Because I want to spend the rest of my life with you.

SARA: Me too.

DAN: That's why I asked you to marry me.

SARA: And that's why I said yes.

At this point, Reid, I'm thinking, oh my god this thing is the worst writer I've ever read. You're a supercomputer—how are you not moving things along faster?? Anyway, it went on—

DAN: So we're on the same page?

SARA: Absolutely.

DAN: Great. Then there's nothing we can't tell each other, right?

SARA: Right.

DAN: Good. Because secrets can be dangerous, don't you think?

SARA: Yes, they can.

DAN: Good. Then you won't mind if I ask you something?

SARA: No, go ahead.

DAN: Who is Paul?

And finally I'm like, "Aha!" GPT-4 says Sara has another man in her life. Great! That's something to work with. But I think a common affair or "lover from her past" or whatever would seem super-predictable. So I try to steer GPT-4 toward something more novel:

Prompt: Continue this scene, but make sure Paul is *not* someone with whom Sara is having an affair. Nor is he a hidden family member, or a former boyfriend, or someone from her job. Her secret about Paul is something different and more unusual. Go!

GPT-4:

SARA: (shocked) Paul? How do you know about Paul?

DAN: I saw the text message on your phone. It said "I miss you, Sara. Can we talk soon?"

SARA: (sighs) Dan, I can explain. Paul is . . . he's . . .

DAN: He's what? Your ex? Your lover? Your brother?

SARA: No, no, no. Nothing like that.

DAN: Then what is he?

SARA: He gave me something very precious and important.

DAN: What did he give you?

SARA: He gave me . . . his kidney.

Did not see that coming!! And now, there's at least the beginning of a story I actually want to know about. A story that I had a real role in shaping (directing GPT-4 to produce a non-obvious twist), but did not per se "write" myself. So I keep bushwhacking through GPT-4's abysmal dialogue (which, granted, I could give directions to fix—"more compact, faster, less like a C-grade soap opera") because now I'm on the hunt for a plot, and GPT-4? GPT-4 is my truffle pig. It keeps writing:

SARA: Five years ago, before I met you, I was diagnosed with a rare genetic disease that caused my kidneys to fail. I needed a transplant urgently. I was on dialysis and waiting for a miracle.

DAN: That's terrible, Sara.

SARA: Thank you, Dan. *[Ughhh!! Stoppp!!!]* But then the miracle happened. A stranger contacted me through a website called Matching Donors. He said he had seen my profile and wanted to help me. He said he was willing to donate one of his kidneys to me anonymously.

DAN: Wow, that's incredible.

SARA: He saved my life.

Then GPT-4 pauses. Like it wants something from me. So I type:

Prompt: Continue the scene. Within the next thirty seconds, reveal why Paul is still in touch with Sara.

GPT-4:

DAN: And then what? Did you keep in touch with him?

SARA: Well, yes and no. We exchanged a few emails and phone calls after the surgery, to check on each other's recovery. He had his own life and I had mine. Until last month. He said he had been diagnosed with cancer.

DAN: Cancer?

SARA: In his remaining kidney. He needed another transplant, and asked me if I could help him find him a donor or raise some money or spread the word.

DAN: And what did you say?

SARA: I said I would do anything I could to help him. How could I not?

Now is this the greatest idea you've ever heard? No. But it's a serviceable, arguably novel plot twist: at least maybe a potential starting point for a movie premise. You can quickly imagine a rom-com version or a psycho-thriller one . . . What if Paul's best kidney-match turns out to be Dan? And what if Dan and Sara aren't engaged just yet, and deep-in-love Dan wants to close the deal but now can't, unless he grants Sara's wish and gives his kidney to creepy Paul? And then Paul, with a new lease on life, turns out to be in love with Sara and tries to get rid of Dan? And so on.

So maybe now I'd spend some "notebook time" with this premise (I still like to brainstorm long-hand)—play with it, see if it leads anywhere good. Use GPT-4 sometimes, sometimes not. That's still me doing that work, exercising that judgment, feeling or not feeling that tingling "Ooh this is some-

*thing" feeling. But GPT-4 definitely helped get me there—once I helped it.**

* * *

I think that story captures a lot of what LLMs can do for writers, and for creatives generally. Not replacing them—aiding them by extending the reach of their creative powers.

So I was pleased when, in early March, MIT researchers reported[7] that two studies** on generative AI's effects on knowledge work found that writers and programmers both saw *50 percent gains* in productivity with AI, and higher satisfaction to boot. Wharton professor Ethan Mollick called the results "completely unprecedented in modern history."[8]

I asked GPT-4 for further examples of how it might help creatives.

> **Reid:** Give an example (10–17 words each) of how GPT could help improve the creative practices of each of the following types of artists/creators: videogame designer, architect, sculptor, hip-hop choreographer, theatrical lighting designer, and documentary film producer. Be specific about how the artist/creator would use GPT to gain this benefit.
>
> **GPT-4:** Some possible examples are:

---

*   My friend added: *Btw, I also asked GPT-4 to generate a Season 1 arc for a TV show I have in development at a major network. I fed it a single paragraph with the show's basic premise and a few character descriptions. Within two minutes it produced something that . . . well, it wasn't usable—too obvious, clearly drawing on some sort of averaged-out amalgam of existing TV series—and yet, it wasn't so far off the mark that it didn't spur some good thoughts. I don't know exactly how writers rooms will use this thing. But I have no doubt that they will use it.*

**   Before peer review, to be fair.

- Videogame designer: GPT generates engaging dialogue and branching narratives for interactive characters.

- Architect: GPT creates realistic 3D models and renders of buildings based on sketches and specifications.

- Sculptor: GPT analyzes the shape, texture, and material of existing sculptures and proposes new variations and combinations.

-Hip-hop choreographer: GPT synthesizes new moves and sequences based on the music, style, and theme of the dance.

-Theatrical lighting designer: GPT simulates different lighting effects and moods for scenes and transitions based on the script and music.

-Documentary film producer: GPT finds relevant facts, sources, and quotes to support the film's thesis and narrative.

Reid: GPT can create 3D models? I thought it was just text output. Similarly: GPT can "synthesize moves"? How? Where is the output I can see?

GPT-4: There are different versions and applications of GPT that can produce different types of output, such as image generation, data analysis, or code writing. Similarly, there are other GPT models that can specialize in generating 3D models, lighting effects, or audio editing, based on text input or other modalities. For example, DALL-E is a GPT-3 variant that can create images from text descriptions, while Jukebox is a neural network that can generate music and lyrics. These models are not perfect, but they demonstrate the potential of GPTs to help improve the creative practices of various types of artists and creators.

And then, this minor *wow* moment: GPT-4, of its own "volition" (if we can speak of such a thing), added something I didn't ask for but that it correctly inferred I would want to know.

GPT-4: To make the examples more realistic and specific, we could add some details about how the artists and creators would use these GPT-based tools or platforms in their workflows. For example:

- Videogame designer: The designer uses a GPT-based dialogue generator to create engaging dialogue and branching narratives for interactive characters. The generator takes into account the character's personality, background, and relationship with the player, as well as the game's genre, setting, and plot. The designer can review and edit the generated dialogue, or provide feedback to improve it.

- Architect: The architect uses a GPT-based 3D modeling software to create realistic 3D models and renders of buildings based on sketches and specifications. The software interprets the sketches and specifications and generates high-quality models that match the architect's vision and style. The software also allows the architect to modify and refine the models, as well as view them from different angles and perspectives.

- Sculptor: The sculptor uses a GPT-based sculpture generator to analyze the shape, texture, and material of existing sculptures and propose new variations and combinations. The generator scans the sculptures and generates novel forms that are inspired by or contrast with them. The sculptor can select and manipulate the generated forms, or use them as inspiration for their own creations.

. . . and so on.

Of course, at this writing, much of this is still hypothetical, or at least not widely available. But I do know enough about tech to be confident that GPT will be the next technology platform—on a scale like the internet, and very possibly bigger—on which the world will build applications, tools, and services of these sorts and literally a million others. And it's going to happen fast, not least because GPT tools will themselves accelerate the development of all the rest of it.

So yes, I'm excited. As a humanist, it's hard to express how excited about this technology I am.

At the same time, I am—just as GPT-4 suggested—not without skepticism. That led me to the following exchange, along with a request for GPT-4 to lighten up its style a touch:

> **Reid:** GPT-4, once large language models are fully developed and deployed, what would you suspect will be the worst effects on the quality of overall cultural production? (200 words) (less wooden style than usual)
>
> **GPT-4:** Large language models, if fully developed and deployed, could have several negative effects on the quality of overall cultural production, such as:
>
> - Homogenization and loss of diversity: Large language models could generate massive amounts of content that mimic existing styles, genres, and trends, but lack originality, creativity, and authenticity. This could result in a saturation of the cultural market with bland and repetitive products that appeal to the lowest common denominator and discourage innovation and experimentation.
>
> - Manipulation and deception: Large language models could also be used to create deceptive or harmful content that exploits human biases, emotions, and

preferences. This could include fake news, propaganda, misinformation, deepfakes, scams, or hate speech that undermine trust, democracy, and social cohesion.

- Displacement and devaluation: Large language models could also pose a threat to human creators and workers in the cultural sector, who could face competition from cheaper, faster, and more scalable AI systems. Large language models could also devalue the cultural value and significance of human-made content by reducing it to mere data and algorithms that can be easily replicated or modified.

Reid: Those are bad! What key steps would you recommend that we as a society take to avoid or minimize these problems? (200 words) (same style as above)

GPT-4: To avoid or minimize these problems, we as a society could take some key steps, such as:

- We could establish and enforce ethical and legal standards and guidelines for the development and use of large language models in the cultural sector, to ensure that it respects human rights, dignity, and diversity, and that it does not harm or deceive consumers or creators. We could also create mechanisms for transparency, accountability, and auditability of large language models and their outputs, to prevent misuse, abuse, or error.

- We could also educate and empower consumers and creators to be aware of the potential benefits and risks of large language models in the cultural sector, and to develop critical and creative skills to evaluate, use, and produce content with or without AI assistance. We could also foster a culture of media literacy, digital citizenship, and information hygiene that promotes responsible and ethical consumption and creation of content.

- And we could support and recognize human creators and workers in the cultural sector, by providing them with adequate resources, opportunities, and incentives to pursue their artistic and professional goals. We could also celebrate and encourage human creativity, diversity, and expression as sources of cultural richness and innovation.

We can't say on the one hand that AI will massively change the world and then that the antidote is "celebrating creativity." Festivals and ribbons aren't going to help put (real) food on (real) tables. As we think about how AI will affect creators, we're going to need some very creative thinking on an economic and policy level too.

Let's get back to a question we put a pin in earlier: who owns this stuff?

> **Reid:** If someone uses this GPT to help generate story ideas, and then she uses one of those ideas to create a screenplay and sells that screenplay, does OpenAI have any claim on the money from the sale? (250 words or less) (make prose more lively and less wooden than usual)

> **GPT-4:** The short answer is: no. OpenAI is a research organization that develops and shares artificial intelligence tools for the benefit of humanity. It does not claim any ownership or rights over the content that its tools produce or help produce. You are free to use the GPT tool as a source of inspiration, but you are responsible for your own originality, quality, and legality of your work.

> The long answer is: it depends. OpenAI has a Terms of Use and an Acceptable Use Policy that govern how you can use its tools and services. You have to agree to these terms when you access the GPT tool, and they include some restrictions and obligations. For example, you cannot use the tool for illegal, harmful, or abusive pur-

poses, or infringe on the rights of others. You also have to acknowledge that the tool may generate inaccurate, offensive, or inappropriate content, and that you are solely liable for any consequences of using or relying on it. You also have to give credit to OpenAI and the GPT tool when you use its output publicly.

So, as long as you follow these terms and respect the copyright and privacy of others, you can use the GPT tool to spark your imagination and create your own stories. But don't forget: the tool is not a substitute for your own creativity, skill, and judgment. You still have to write your own screenplay, polish it, sell it, and hope that it becomes a hit. And if it does, you can enjoy the fruits of your labor without worrying about OpenAI knocking on your door.

That's, legitimately, good news.

But what about the flip side of artists using GPT-4—what about when GPT-4 uses artists? What happens when an LLM or image generator like Dall-E incorporates artists' online IP into its learning, perhaps without the artist's explicit permission? As the *New York Times* reported in February:

> "Artists are afraid of posting new art," the computer science professor Ben Zhao said. Putting art online is how many artists advertise their services but now they have a "fear of feeding this monster that becomes more and more like them," Professor Zhao said. "It shuts down their business model."

This strikes me as a reasonable concern, and Professor Zhao's solution—Glaze, a tool for artists to digitally "mask" their images—seems a reasonable, and creative, response. Glaze changes an image at a pixel level that the human eye can't perceive, but that a 'bot "understands" as an entirely different style of image:

> . . . that Stable Diffusion would associate with, for example, the splattered paint blobs of Jackson Pollock. . . . When [artist Karla] Ortiz posted her Glazed work online, an image generator trained on those images wouldn't be able to mimic her work. A prompt with her name would instead lead to images in some hybridized style of her works and Pollock's. "We're taking our consent back," Ms. Ortiz said.

It's an early example of what's sure to be a dynamic and sometimes contentious relationship between creators and AI. But then, creators' relations to tech innovation have always been complicated. At the mid-19th-century advent of photography, painters had legitimate concerns. Some careers surely were disrupted—and both painters and photographers have been doing incredible creative work ever since.

Of course there are many, many other ways GPTs will be relevant to our creative futures. To get a sense for the scope, I naturally asked GPT-4. (By now I'd gotten good at remembering to ask it to write in a more enjoyable style than its default.)

> **Reid:** For a book about the future of GPT, outline a chapter about GPT's impact on creative work and cultural production. Don't cover the basics of what GPT is or how it works, as that will be covered in earlier chapters. Include good and bad potentials. Outline should be 200 words or less. Write for a college-educated but non-specialist audience. Slightly breezy in style.

GPT-4: Chapter X: GPT and the Creative Economy

Introduction: GPT is not only a powerful tool for generating text, but also for creating images, music, video, and other forms of media. How will this affect the creative work and cultural production of humans and machines? What are the opportunities and challenges for artists, consumers, and society at large?

- Section 1: GPT as a creative assistant: How GPT can help human creators with tasks such as brainstorming, editing, feedback, translation, and marketing. Examples of successful collaborations between GPT and human artists, such as OpenAI's Jukebox, DALL-E, and MuseNet. The benefits of augmenting human creativity with artificial intelligence, such as enhancing diversity, accessibility, and innovation.

- Section 2: GPT as a creative competitor: How GPT can also generate original and high-quality content without human input or supervision. Examples of autonomous GPT creations, such as Philosopher AI, This X Does Not Exist, and AIDungeon. The risks of displacing human creators, undermining intellectual property, and eroding artistic value. The ethical and legal implications of AI authorship and ownership.

- Section 3: GPT as a creative catalyst: How GPT can also inspire new forms of creative expression and cultural participation. Examples of hybrid and interactive GPT projects, such as Botnik Studios, GPT-3 Poetry, and NovelAI. The potential of fostering co-creation, remixing, and experimentation among human and machine agents. The challenges of ensuring quality, authenticity, and responsibility in the emerging creative economy.

- Conclusion: GPT is transforming the landscape of creative work and cultural production in unprecedented ways. It invites us to rethink our roles and relationships in the dynamic interplay between humans and machines.

Couldn't have said it better myself.

JUSTICE

IN THE FALL OF 2022, WHILE THE topics of this book and AI in general were very much top-of-mind for me, I visited the Legacy Museum at the Equal Justice Initiative (EJI) in Montgomery, Alabama. Bryan Stevenson, EJI's founder and Executive Director, is someone I respect and admire very much. His view, with which I agree, is that we should judge our moral character and nobility as a society by how we treat the poor, the disenfranchised, and the powerless.

An equal, effective justice system is a basic prerequisite for achieving our highest potential. We cannot hope to lift up one portion of society while leaving others behind, and as such, the basic concept of justice has been vitally important to me for a long time.

For us to simply say of slavery, "That was the past, and now we are fine" is badly self-deceptive and destructive, and to be reminded of slavery's tangible evil through the hard but necessary work of people like Bryan and others at EJI is a necessary part of combating its aftermath.

Located near one of the most infamous slave auction sites in the U.S., the Legacy Museum does a spectacular job of reminding us how the lasting effects of this particular form of cruelty, torture, and economic exploitation echoes in our history.

As the Legacy Museum demonstrates, the 20th-century emergence of over-incarceration is one of slavery's most enduring artifacts. In her truly excellent book, *The New Jim Crow,* Michelle Alexander reveals the horrifying fact that more Black men are involved in the American carceral system today—whether physically incarcerated, on parole, or on probation—than were enslaved in 1850.

This is a gross injustice that we must strive to fix, and frankly, I wouldn't be as excited about GPT-4 as I am if I didn't think it could help do just that.

A necessary conversation

A few caveats before we dive in:

I want to note that my focus in this chapter is mostly on the U.S. For starters, that is where I live and do much of my work, but also, as mentioned above, the sad reality is that the U.S. has one of the highest incarceration rates in the world.

I also want to acknowledge that, as a privileged white American man, there are many limitations to my perspective. In addition, I recognize that talking about potential positive AI use cases in the realm of criminal justice is charged, precisely because historically this is a domain where AI has been problematic. But the fact is that this is already happening—AI is here, it's already being used, and it's not going away.

Now it is up to us to decide how these technologies will be used, and whether we get a say in how they are applied in the context of criminal justice. If we don't engage in that conversation, we risk ceding the development and even the definition of what these tools can be to the institutions that have historically put structural inequalities into place. Is that a risk we want to take?

No matter how difficult the conversation, I believe it would be negligent not to discuss the ways in which AI can be used to give us more justice, not less. We will never get it perfect—there will always be some biases inherent in any human system—but we must keep striving toward better.

Where things can go wrong

The problems with any existing or potential deployment of AI in a criminal justice setting are well-documented. Just the concept has such dystopian potential that it has inspired multitudes of sci-fi movies and books—but you don't need to look to fiction to see where AI usage in criminal justice can and has gone awry.

Critics of predictive policing, for example, fear that human bias will be "baked in"—which has definitely already happened.[9] This bias is then reified by the AI algorithm's seeming authority, which, even more than a judge, might appear to be an "objective" decision maker.

Facial recognition algorithms have also been problematic, resulting in multiple studies showing higher false positive rates[10] on darker-skinned individuals.

I could go on, but my point here is not to dwell on the downsides, whether potential or actual.

Instead, I think one of the most promising things about GPT-4, and the way OpenAI designed it to be used, is that it is putting AI's power into the hands of individual citizens in the hope of empowering them in grassroots, decentralized, democratic ways.

So that's the lens I'd like to look through here. How can we use AI to empower individuals or communities that have traditionally been marginalized and targeted by state power—including state power *enabled by* AI—and develop ways to proactively use AI to deliver justice in new ways?

Body-worn cameras

Let's start with cameras—in particular, the recent call for all police officers to use body-worn cameras (BWCs). Statistics from 2018[11] suggest that nearly half of U.S. law enforcement agencies are already using body-worn cameras in some way, with that number closer to 80 percent for large police departments.

As the ACLU[12] says, body-worn cameras "serve as a much-needed police oversight tool at a time of a growing recognition that the United States has a real problem with police violence . . . [but] without good policies, they risk becoming just another police surveillance device—and one with very real potential to invade privacy."

Again, here we see real benefits to society balanced with equally real risks. How can we lean into the former while mitigating the effects of the latter?

> **Reid:** How should we be thinking about the potential benefits and risks of body-worn cameras used in policing?

> **GPT-4:** Potential benefits of body-worn cameras in policing include improved transparency, accountability, and trust between officers and the public, as well as a deterrent for potentially aggressive behavior. Body-worn cameras also provide a valuable source of evidence for criminal investigations.

However, there are potential risks associated with body-worn cameras. These include privacy concerns, data security issues, and the potential for increased surveillance of vulnerable populations. Furthermore, the technology can be expensive and require a significant amount of staff training and resources. Therefore, it is important to weigh the potential benefits and risks of body-worn cameras carefully before introducing them into a policing environment.

Reid: How can AI play a role in maximizing these benefits while preventing some of the risks?

GPT-4: There are a number of ways that AI could play a role in maximizing the benefits and preventing risks associated with body-worn cameras:

- AI-powered video analytics could help to automatically identify and redact sensitive or personally identifiable information in footage captured by body-worn cameras. This would help to protect the privacy of individuals captured on video.

- AI could help to automate the process of reviewing footage and identifying key moments or events, saving time for law enforcement officers and making it easier to extract valuable evidence from the footage.

- AI could also help to detect instances of officer misconduct or use of force, potentially assisting in the identification and investigation of such incidents.

- Finally, AI could be used to analyze trends and patterns in the footage captured by body-worn cameras, helping to improve training and policies around the use of this technology.

That all sounds promising, but given the potential downsides, it will still take human intention and direction to make sure these technologies are put to good use.

One new company whose work I'm particularly excited about is JusticeText. (Full disclosure: I'm an angel investor in the company, alongside Bloomberg Beta, Michael Tubbs, John Legend, and many others).

Led by Devshi Mehrotra, JusticeText makes software that helps public defenders analyze and share video evidence to ensure their clients have the same access to this evidence as the prosecution. The product automatically transcribes and tags video data, making it easier for attorneys to use in court.

The company is still in start-up mode, but they are working with over fifty public defender offices and sixty private attorneys, with plans to continue scaling up. Their belief—which I support wholeheartedly—is that their AI technology can help more defendants get the justice they deserve.

Legal services

After you've spent time with GPT-4, you see that it's very good at generating text in specific formats. That text can take whatever format you want, be it song lyrics or—more relevant here—court briefings and motions.

It shouldn't be controversial to say that the quality of legal representation people in the U.S. get depends on the size of their bank account. In that context, it's not hard to see how many of our country's less well-to-do defendants could be better served using AI, and specifically LLMs like GPT-4.

To my mind, just as GPT-4 could become a copilot for every professional worker, it could also be a copilot for everyone navigating our criminal justice system.

Imagine if every overworked, under-resourced public defender had a trusty GPT-4 assistant at their side to help manage the no-doubt-too-many cases on their plate that month.

Better yet, let's ask GPT-4 to imagine just such a scenario.

Reid: Give me an imaginary scenario in which a public defender uses an AI such as GPT-4 to navigate the legal system. What would that look like?

GPT-4 (edited for length): In the near future, a public defender working in a legal system may have the option to utilize an AI such as GPT-4 to improve their productivity and accuracy. By using such an AI, the public defender would be able to quickly assess cases and determine the best course of action for their clients.

The AI may be used to quickly search through cases in legal databases for relevant information, facts, and details. It could also be used to recommend legal strategies or tactics for the ongoing case. In some instances, its applications could even go beyond the traditional attorney-client relationship and provide advice on the best way to present a case in court or deal with complicated legal matters.

Using an AI for such purposes could also work towards improving access to justice. People who are unfamiliar with the complexities of the legal system could find it easier to understand the proceedings due to the AI's intuitive design and user-friendly interface. This could be especially beneficial for those who live in remote or rural areas where legal services may be scarce.

What a huge difference having access to those services could make for people traditionally underserved by the legal system—many of whom[13] are being wrongfully convicted due to police and other official misconduct.

Prisons, education, & recidivism

In this ultra-connected day and age, where technical proficiency is a key life- and job skill, internet access in prison remains extremely limited. Even when prisons do allow access to the outer world, it is highly regulated—i.e., sending emails only to family members that are on a pre-approved list. In this way, prisons hope to deter negative behaviors by denying more access to people and information outside of prison.

Another defining aspect of life in prison—and how many people arrive there—is poor literacy. Studies show[14] that 75 percent of U.S. prisoners are illiterate, and two-thirds of students[15] who cannot read proficiently by the end of the fourth grade will end up in jail or on welfare.

Finally, life in prison is isolated and idle, which itself can catalyze a myriad of negative outcomes: mental health and/or behavioral issues, suicide, violence, recidivism, etc.

I think GPT-4 can be of huge benefit in many of these scenarios.

> **Reid:** Please list for me the ways in which GPT-4 and similar AIs could be of help with counteracting illiteracy, recidivism, and loneliness among a prison population.

> **GPT-4 (edited for length):** GPT-4 and similar AIs can be of great help in countering illiteracy, recidivism, and loneliness among a prison population in the following ways:

- Providing inmates with access to educational materials such as e-books, videos, and podcasts, which could help improve their literacy levels.

- Introducing virtual mentors, who could help inmates develop better social skills, build meaningful relationships, and create career pathways for themselves.

- Connecting inmates with online communities of others who have been through similar experiences. This could reduce feelings of loneliness and isolation, as well as provide encouragement and support.

And, if the main concern of prison connectivity is the supervisory burden of overseeing interactions between inmates and the outside world, GPT-4 could reduce or even eliminate that need.

I'm a proud supporter of Ameelio, a not-for-profit company that democratizes prison communication and education technology by providing free letters and phone calls for incarcerated individuals as well as providing the technology to bring updated, high-quality education materials into prisons and jails. They believe, and I agree, that by providing incarcerated people with support networks and vital resources, we can cut recidivism and sustainably reduce prison populations.

It is impossible not to be excited about how GPT-4 could be used to help an organization like Ameelio reach more people who are currently incarcerated in a more cost-effective, impactful way. With 95 percent of those who are currently incarcerated slated to re-enter society, it is not only our moral obligation to think about how we can help these individuals, but will also be of massive benefit to our society at large.

White-collar crime

While thus far I've mostly been focused on so-called "blue-collar crime," I also think AI can be helpful in catching white-collar criminals. These crimes tend to be less visceral, so they get less attention in the media, but that is not at all in proportion to their massive impact on society.

Whether it's corporate crime, Ponzi schemes, or price collusion (to name a few examples), white-collar crime costs the U.S. over $300 billion each year, according to the FBI. These types of crime are harder to detect and prosecute because they often involve business or financial leaders, who can disguise their activities or may seem above reproach due to their reputation. Bernie Madoff was chairman of the Nasdaq stock exchange in the early '90s—who would have suspected him of committing crimes of such magnitude?

Well, an AI might have.

> **Reid:** GPT-4, I'm curious: do you think an AI would have been able to catch Bernie Madoff sooner than people did?

> **GPT-4:** Yes, it's possible that an AI would have been able to catch Bernie Madoff sooner than people did. AI systems can analyze data more quickly than humans and can detect patterns that are too subtle for the human eye to recognize. In the case of Bernie Madoff, the AI could have spotted certain discrepancies in his financial records that were missed by human investigators. In addition, AI systems are not as susceptible to manipulation or distraction, so they would have been able to stay on track and focus on uncovering any suspicious activity.

That last point is a key reason I believe that AI can be especially effective in combating white-collar crime, saving us as a country billions every year.

Toward a more perfect system

I believe that we can use AI to amplify our own humanity, our own compassion, our own intelligence, and create a better, more fair criminal justice system.

Note that my goal here is to create a *better* system, not a *perfect* one. We will never get our justice system perfectly right, because there are humans in the loop. We will always have some biases, some errors, some imperfections.

Yet that doesn't mean we don't try. We should all care deeply about fixing this system, so riddled with injustices. Let's strive to get it as close to perfect as we can, acknowledging that we must do so in a cost-effective manner that is attainable with our policy goals and realistic for our society. What I don't want is for any hint of imperfection to sidetrack us from our goal.

And, as I stated at the start of this chapter, I recognize my own limitations in discussing criminal justice reform. That's one of the reasons why I value talking to experts in the field like Bryan Stevenson, who has graciously agreed to be on my podcast, *Possible*. Bryan has dedicated his life's work to this topic, and I'm looking forward to learning from and sharing his perspective on all of these issues in a deeper and more nuanced manner than is possible here.

JOURNALISM

FOR THE AMERICAN JOURNALISM INDUSTRY, IT'S BEEN twenty years of mostly bad news. With the rise of the internet, competition for ad dollars from non-news players has destroyed the industry's traditional business models—even as participation from a public that, finally empowered to talk back, has slowly eroded journalism's authority.

Newspaper publishers—which have traditionally done the heavy lifting of holding power accountable and informing the public about current affairs—have suffered the worst of it. According to the Pew Research Center,[16] more than 2,200 local U.S. papers have closed since 2005, and over 40,000 newsroom employees have lost their jobs.

Meanwhile, we keep producing more and more information. Like, a *lot* of it:

> **Reid:** Can you quantify how much information the world produces each day in 2022? Also, can you provide any statistics that help illustrate how fast this overall information production is growing over time? Finally, I'd like to use your reply as part of an argument I'm making that large language models can play a significant positive role in the journalism industry. So please don't make stuff up. Base your reply on real sources that can be easily checked.

GPT-4: According to a report by the International Data Corporation (IDC), the world is expected to produce about 175 zettabytes of data by 2025, which is equivalent to 175 trillion gigabytes. This means that the average daily data creation in 2025 would be about 479.5 billion gigabytes. Assuming a linear growth rate from 2020 to 2025, the average daily data creation in 2022 would be about 374.4 exabytes, or 374.4 billion gigabytes.

To put this number in perspective, one exabyte of data is enough to store about 250 million DVDs, or to stream Netflix for eighty-six million years.

For the record, I fact-checked this reply and it appears to be correct. We're now producing approximately 375 billion gigabytes of data per day.

Naturally, only a small percentage of this data is newsworthy.

If we're to achieve any degree of clarity in this world of information superabundance— to effectively set priorities and maintain accountability—we need institutions that can effectively aggregate, summarize, analyze, and generally make sense of this daily data tsunami.

For journalism, with its long institutional experience in storytelling, error-correction, contextualizing, and overall truth-seeking, this represents both a huge challenge and a massive opportunity.

I believe the industry is up to that challenge, but only if its most responsible and ambitious practitioners adopt tools that can dramatically amplify the efforts and impacts of their human employees. To me, that means embracing tools like GPT-4 sooner rather than later.

I asked GPT-4 to generate a "travel advisory" for a dystopian 2032, where new AI technologies enable large-scale disinformation:

Reid: Imagine it's 2032, in the months leading up to the U.S. presidential election. Thanks to new AI technologies, fake news at scale pollutes the massive quantities of information we as a society now produce. It's truly a dystopian hellscape. There are fake celebrity endorsements of candidates. False confessions from candidates. Manipulated real-time debates streaming at the same time the real debates are happening. A hologram of Jesus in a MAGA cap, showing up on stage at political rallies. Write a 150-word "travel advisory" for potential voters seeking news and information they can use to help guide the choices they will ultimately make on Election Day.

GPT-4: Possible travel advisory: Attention voters: You are about to enter a dangerous zone of misinformation, deception, and manipulation. The AI-powered fake news industry is working overtime to influence your vote and undermine your democracy. Do not trust any source of information without verifying its credibility, authenticity, and accuracy. Beware of deepfakes, synthetic voices, holograms, and other forms of digital trickery that can create realistic but false images and sounds. Use fact-checking tools, independent media outlets, and your own critical thinking skills to distinguish between facts and fiction. Do not share or spread any content that you are not sure is true or that could harm others. Seek out diverse and respectful perspectives from different sources and communities. Remember, your vote is your voice, and it matters. Do not let the fake news win. Stay informed, stay safe, and stay engaged.

"Holy crap!" you may be saying right now. "The prompt was *hologram MAGA Jesus*, and GPT-4 thinks the antidote is 'critical thinking'?"

Unfortunately, when it comes to ensuring that truth has a future, the simple answer is that there are no simple answers.

But, optimist that I am, I see at least three clear steps we can take to help preserve society's capacity for truth-seeking:

1) Truth-seeking institutions must learn to work faster.

2) Truth-seeking institutions must engage audiences better.

3) Truth-seeking institutions must "flood the zone" with truth.

The common denominator in achieving these steps? I believe it's AI.

Accelerate the presses!

Ask a journalist the value that most shapes their work and there's a good chance they'll say "accuracy" (especially if they're talking on the record). But there's a reason journalism is often described as "the first rough draft of history": in journalism, as in many industries, speed matters.

Whether journalists are reporting on wars, political campaigns, weather events, market conditions, or an extremely popular new restaurant, they're forever battling the clock to gather information as quickly as they can to deliver some working theory of the truth to their audiences.

Sometimes, this imperative of speed means that journalists' rough drafts of history are rough indeed. Context goes missing. Important aspects of a story have not yet surfaced.

So while most of us may think of journalism as a *product*, it's ultimately a *process*—iterative and self-correcting. Ideally, tomorrow's stories refine, clarify, and expand on today's. Accuracy is a persistent defining value, but so is speed.

That's a major reason I believe GPT-4 and other AI tools will have such an outsized, net-positive impact on journalism: they'll help news organizations gather, produce, and distribute the news faster than ever before.

This includes automatically sifting through massive troves of public records to find the important stories hidden within. It means monitoring and analyzing 800+ million social media posts a day to do the same. It means generating headlines and transcribing interviews in seconds, and packaging and personalizing the same basic information into many different styles and formats.

"AYFKM?!" I imagine some journalist reader is acronyming right now. "You want to use GPT-4, which definitely still has that pesky side effect of *making shit up*, to *amplify* journalism's misguided mandate to be first more than factual? Half-baked and half-right? If it speeds, it leads?"

Hold your tweets, please. That's not what I mean.

Moving forward, good journalism will still require painstaking work and judicious but urgent human discernment and assessment. Good journalism will still require a prudent, thorough, multi-stage editorial process. That's not changing any time soon. Sometimes, the process won't actually be that fast. Sometimes (just like before AI), it won't be error-free.

However, as I suggested above, speed has always informed the journalistic process. In fact, because of this need for speed, good journalism has always quickly adopted and then effectively leveraged great technology, including printing presses, cameras, tape recorders, TV networks, the internet, and smartphones, all of which accelerated and amplified the production and distribution of news.

Now it's happening again. Overall, AI tools will help journalists work more productively and more effectively.

As for GPT-4's capacity to hallucinate,* journalists should obviously take special care regarding this aspect of GPT-4 and review its outputs accordingly. Powerful tools always require higher standards of attention and expertise, whether it's cars, chainsaws, or complex algorithms. It's the price these tools charge for the productivity they deliver.

Besides, with the ongoing rapid evolution of LLMs, in a year or two, the rates at which they generate hallucinations are likely to be much lower than they are now.

In the meantime, given how GPT-4 can potentially amplify news organizations' overall productivity, I believe the vigilance required to manage GPT-4's (undeniable) current shortcomings is a smart investment for them to make. In fact, journalism's long-established culture of verification and correction are perfectly suited to the task.

Question authoritatively

In one of the first prompts I entered when I started researching this chapter, I asked GPT-4 to "summarize some of the

---

*   Discussed at length in "When AI Makes Things Up ("Hallucinations")" most prominent instances over the last ten years where AI-assisted reporting helped a news organization break an important story."

This quickly yielded some very specific and in-depth information, but it also included some errors. Knowing what I know about GPT-4—it sometimes makes things up—I knew I'd need to check this information against other sources, and Google and Wikipedia certainly played a useful role in this part of the process.

In the end, though, the key to getting me up to speed here was GPT-4. While the information it had provided was partially wrong, it was also *mostly* right. And, most importantly, GPT-4 produced this information extremely quickly.

When I'd Googled the same kind of information, it offered me dozens of links, some of which looked promising, others not. The Wikipedia experience differed in details but not in results.

With GPT-4, though, its capacity to instantly synthesize information from a wide range of sources meant that I received exactly the kind of list I'd been envisioning within seconds.

This list contained errors, but that was OK because—and this is a key point—*I wasn't looking for or expecting a finished product.* I was looking for an informed starting point, a rough map of the territory I wanted to explore, to help me quickly get a sense of which questions I should be asking.

Having thus oriented myself, I then spent a fair amount of time querying GPT-4 about the ways that the Associated Press, Reuters, the *Washington Post*, *Bloomberg News*, the *Guardian*, the *New York Times*, and others have incorporated AI into their newsgathering, production, distribution, and business functions—far more time than I'd planned to spend, to be honest.

That's because interacting with GPT-4 is not like traditional web searching. Instead, it's better evoked by a term that was popular back in the early days of Web 1.0: web surfing. A dialogue develops. A flow state takes over. You ask GPT-4 a question and it responds right away with highly relevant information, not just a series of links.

So then you immediately think of more questions and ask those. Thus the process of discovery that can often feel halting and frustrating using traditional search methods— "Oh, I guess that link isn't really about AI and journalism at all . . ."— feels more like steady progress toward greater awareness and understanding.

This, I believe, is a huge part of what's fueling the immense popularity of GPT-4's sibling, ChatGPT. The experience itself is so responsive and self-propelling that a kind of intellectual escalation kicks in: asking one question makes you want to ask ten.

This phenomenon, I also realized, was a big part of the story I should tell in this chapter. Initially, I had assumed that I would highlight automated journalism, describing how news organizations are already using databases and template-driven AI systems to produce thousands of stories about corporate earnings reports, weather forecasts, sports events, and more. But while automated journalism does represent a strategic opportunity for news organizations, conversing with GPT-4 took me down a different path.

The story I found most compelling in terms of its potential impact on the journalism industry is how GPT-4 itself can increase consumers' engagement. People are going to like news more when they have more control over how it's delivered—and, as a result, I suspect they'll want more of it.

Extra! Extra! Ask all about it!

Delivering highly personalized user experiences has driven internet development for more than thirty years. Platforms like YouTube, Facebook, and Amazon all keep close tabs on the content you consume, then use it to recommend more content they think you will like. (Not to mention the pair of sneakers you first looked at two years ago that continues to follow you from website to website like a lost, lonely puppy.)

News media websites use personalization, too, and as I continued to submit various questions to GPT-4 about AI's potential impact on journalism, "personalization" was a recurring theme.

When I asked GPT-4 how this personalization would work, here's what it replied:

> **Reid:** To make news media websites more personalized, what data will these websites use to analyze readers' behavior and preferences?

> **GPT-4:** News media websites will use data such as the reader's location, the type of device they are using, their browsing history, and the articles they have previously read or interacted with. They can also analyze which articles the reader has shared on social media, how long they spend on the website, and which sections they visit most frequently. Additionally, data on the reader's age, gender, and interests can be used to personalize content. This data can be obtained through cookies, surveys, and user accounts, among other methods. By analyzing

this data, news media websites can tailor their content to the reader's preferences and interests, providing a more personalized experience.

In other words, the traditional approach. Not too innovative.

Meanwhile, as I noted above, the "conversational chat" approach that GPT-4 and especially its sibling ChatGPT were themselves using offered its own powerful—but significantly different—version of personalization.

In contrast to how traditional web-based personalization works, with websites perpetually surveilling users over time, GPT-4 and ChatGPT simply offer highly responsive information to your queries and prompts in real-time. This is both a somewhat obvious observation about how these LLMs operate, but also (as yet) an under-appreciated one.

Indeed, it's not just their human-like fluency and seeming expertise on so many subjects that makes them so popular. Unlike chatbots designed to promote a product or politician, GPT-4 and ChatGPT are not only able but also incredibly willing to focus on whatever you want to talk about.* This simple dynamic creates a highly personalized user experience. As an exchange with GPT-4 progresses, you are continuously fine-tuning it to your specific preferences in that moment. While this high degree of personalization informs whatever you're using GPT-4 for, I believe it has special salience for the news media industry.

Imagine a future where you go to a news website and use queries like these to define your experience there:

---

* Provided it doesn't violate the safety restrictions OpenAI has put on them.

- Hey, *Wall Street Journal*, give me hundred-word summaries of your three most-read tech stories today.

- Hey, *CNN*, show me any climate change stories that happened today involving policy-making.

- Hey, *New York Times*, can you create a counter-argument to today's Paul Krugman op-ed, using only news articles from your archives as its sources?

- Hey, *USA Today*, please point me toward any stories today that would be interesting to professional educators.

- Hey, *Fox News,* can you give me a list of reader comments that are getting the most engagement today?

At the heart of this approach, journalists are still creating the content that serves as the starting point for user experiences. Now, however, users get to take a much more active role in deciding what they consume and how they consume it.

By enabling this functionality on their websites, news organizations can capitalize on the same one-question-begets-ten-questions dynamic driving ChatGPT's growth.

In addition, this functionality would also create new opportunities for trust, which of course is a bilateral phenomenon. While I personally trust many news organizations generally, I also think most news organizations have not done nearly as much as they could do to engage their users more productively—to treat them more like active participants rather than passive consumers. But giving users more power to define their own news consumption pathways would be one genuinely substantive way to do that.

Finally, such functionality would also help news organizations maximize the full value of all the information they've generated over the years. In making this information more accessible and better-integrated into their ongoing efforts, it would likely both increase engagement and also serve as a strong statement about their own transparency and accountability.

In compiling the list of example queries above, I obviously chose some that show how users could effectively fact-check a news organization with its own content—a prospect that might seem self-defeating in an age where millions of internet watchdogs are looking for any chance to howl "FAKE NEWS!" at mainstream news sources.

But transparency and accountability are the true north of any society that aspires to truth-seeking. And, in a world overwhelmed by misinformation, disinformation, and simply too much information, it becomes especially necessary for truth-seekers to live the values they work to preserve.

Rebuilding trust in the 21st century

I saw an article recently that seemed so relevant to AI's potential impact on journalism, I think it's worth including here in full:

> **Putin Claims AI Disinformation Tools Are Weapons of Mass Destruction**
>
> By Anton Troianovski
>
> MOSCOW—President Vladimir V. Putin of Russia, a longtime foe of Western democracies, warned on state TV on Tuesday of a new threat: artificial intelligence technologies that can generate fake news and other disinformation.

Mr. Putin named ChatGPT, DALL-E, and other AI tools that can create realistic texts, images, and videos from a few words, as examples of technologies that can manipulate public opinion, sow discord, and erode trust in reality. "These tools are weapons of mass destruction that can deceive, manipulate, and harm millions of people, not only in our country, but in any country on earth," Mr. Putin said.

Mr. Putin accused the leaders of the U.S. and China, where such technologies are being developed, of having a moral obligation to ban them immediately, and to cooperate with international organizations to prevent their misuse. "If they do not act now, they will be responsible for unleashing a new form of warfare that will endanger the lives and livelihoods of billions of people, and the fate of the planet itself," Mr. Putin said.

Some experts and activists have welcomed Mr. Putin's call for a ban on AI disinformation tools, while others have dismissed it as a cynical and hypocritical attempt to deflect attention from his own record of using such tools and other methods to interfere in other countries and to suppress dissent and criticism at home. They have also questioned his sincerity and credibility, given his history of denying and lying about his involvement in various scandals and controversies.

"Mr. Putin is the last person who should be lecturing the world about the dangers of AI and disinformation, when he is the master of both," said Kulla Kaljulaid, a spokesperson for the Estonian Ministry of Foreign Affairs.

*   *   *

For the record, in case I fooled anyone, I asked GPT-4 to generate this "article." It's fake news.

Obviously, it's nothing a human couldn't write themselves. But it also took me mere seconds to produce—and it barely even scratches the surface of what's possible.

Indeed, of all the potential ways LLMs could negatively impact journalism, disinformation at scale tops the list. Right below that is the potential elimination of journalism jobs. Happily— if that word can be applied here—I believe the first possibility greatly reduces the chances of the second.

How does this play out?

Consider what Steve Bannon famously told journalist Michael Lewis in 2018: "The Democrats don't matter. The real opposition is the media. And the way to deal with them is to flood the zone with shit."

To date, the tendency of LLMs like Bing Chat and ChatGPT to produce inadvertent misinformation in their own faulty attempts to write statistically plausible "truth" has overshadowed their potential use as disinformation fire hoses that bad actors could use to, ahem, muddy the waters of public discourse.

Obviously, that potential is there, waiting patiently.

When bad actors inevitably put these tools to such ends, I'm sure we'll see calls for new regulation tailored specifically to AI-generated disinformation. We may even see efforts to ban some AI technologies entirely. In a globally connected world, though, unilateral disarmament is not a viable strategy.

As this governance process plays out, my chief hope is that legislators and developers try to work together collaboratively, with an emphasis on long-term outcomes rather than reflexive attempts to halt progress in the name of reducing the risk of adverse effects to zero. No babies going out with the bathwater.

However things evolve, I strongly believe that any effective strategy to neutralize disinformation—whether AI-generated or human-made—will involve using AI tools to detect such material.

I also believe it's equally important—possibly even more important—to flood the zone with truth.

What does that mean? Essentially, we have to make accurate, transparent, and truthful information extremely easy to find, for anyone who wants to find it.

In many respects, Wikipedia is a good example of what I'm envisioning here. It's a massive archive of fact-based information, with transparent and rigorously enforced processes for adding and editing the information it contains.

With Wikipedia, more clearly sourced context is always just a click away. You can link to the sources an entry uses as the basis for its narrative. You can see who created an entry and when, who edited it, what specific edits they made, and what other entries they've edited. You can see which edits were contested and why.

All told, Wikipedia makes it easy for users to see and evaluate how it has arrived at the "truths" it presents, and consequently how much they should or should not trust those truths.

Wikipedia leverages the efforts of thousands of volunteer contributors, but they're also largely building on the work of professional news organizations, whose published output serves as the sources for a huge percentage of its entries. Had Wikipedia not been able to use one hundred-plus years of truth-seeking content from thousands of professional news organizations, it would not be the resource it is today.

Of course, Wikipedia is just one site. To flood the zone with truth, we need many entities working toward this end. News organizations can and should play a key role in this effort—which will require innovation and adaptation on their parts.

News organizations know how the growth of disinformation affects their own perceived value. In 2017, CNN began a multi-year marketing campaign declaring its commitment to "Facts First." The *New York Times* has run its own long-term ad campaigns with messages like "The Truth is Hard," and "The Truth is Worth It."

More than marketing, though, we need new processes and formats where verification, context, and accountability can be easily applied in very transparent, persistent, shareable, and easy-to-evaluate ways.

What if every article published on NYTimes.com or FoxNews. com had a "Fact Check" button on it, just as they now have buttons to email or tweet an article?

This new button could trigger an audit from a third-party site equipped with sophisticated AI tools to assess the article on the fly. Are the statistics the article cites verifiable? Appropriately contextualized? Who are the sources it quotes, and what additional information about them would be helpful? How does the story fit into its topic's larger context? What are the sources of any images, video, and audio the article incorporates? Are these elements genuine or synthetic?

Providing this level of scrutiny for every article a news organization publishes might seem like overkill, and maybe it is. Certainly a human-powered system like this would be too time-consuming, too costly, not feasible.

AI gives us new superpowers, however, and we should apply them ambitiously. In a world where hard-to-detect disinformation could mix freely with carefully reported, methodically verified information, we must do everything we can to make the good stuff easy to identify.

What kind of impact might this have?

For starters, it could quickly help sort the world's information into two basic categories: that which proactively encourages evaluation and verification, and that which doesn't.

Of course, the problem with fake news is not just fake news, it's that so many people *want* fake news because it supports what they already believe to be true. Even so, what's the downside to creating a more visible culture of informational transparency and accountability, where the "ingredients" of at least some news articles become as legible and easy to check as the nutrition label on a can of soup?

If thousands of news organizations, including those with explicit ideological perspectives, start flooding the zone with truth in this manner, we could potentially put a real dent in the market for misinformation.

Without journalists, there is no journalism

Throughout this leg of my journey, I've asserted that the spread of AI tools like GPT-4 will create once-in-a-generation opportunities for journalism and journalists.

As I've also alluded to, though, the sticking point here is the current state of the journalism industry. It's hard to embrace risks that lead to growth when you've been stuck so long in survival mode.

And yet, when the need for principled truth-seeking is more pressing than ever, there are clearly opportunities, especially for those who can figure out novel ways to capitalize on new AI tools as they come online. Leveraging new technologies' power is one of the main ways the journalism industry grew in the past, and probably *the* main way it can do so again.

What does this mean for individual journalists who want to stay relevant?

For starters, and perhaps obviously, they should be doing everything they can to familiarize themselves with AI tools like GPT-4, and experimenting with new ways to find and tell stories.

At the same time, it's also true that a constant refrain in GPT-4's thoughts on the growing impact of technology on journalism was its insistence on the need for a human touch. A few examples from our conversations:

GPT-4: AI is a powerful tool that can augment and enhance the work of human journalists, but it should not be relied upon entirely, as it may not have the human judgment and experience required to report on certain topics accurately and ethically.

GPT-4: Human journalists can apply their professional judgment, curiosity, and background knowledge to evaluate sources, data, and information, identify gaps, biases, and errors, and generate original insights, angles, and questions that AI tools may not be able to do or may miss.

GPT-4: It's important to note, however, that AI-generated headlines and captions should still be reviewed and approved by human editors, to ensure that they are factually accurate, ethically sound, and in line with the tone and values of the news organization.

Sure, it's possible to read these utterances as blandly collegial brushoffs from a shrewdly flattering machine intelligence. That's the cynical take.

I, for one, see so much truth in GPT-4's responses. Journalism is a very human business. It demands and rewards curiosity, creativity, a strong ethical compass, and, at its best, a commitment to fact told through a lens of empathy.

There are simple practical matters in play, too. GPT-4 can't go to the scene of a fire and start asking questions. It doesn't know how to find a potential source at the statehouse and gain their trust over time. It lacks the moral reasoning and contextual understanding that come from living in the world, as a human.

In the end, then, my hope here is two-fold. First, I hope journalists will actively, even aggressively, incorporate tools like GPT-4 to amplify their efforts and make them more productive.

And second, I hope in doing so that journalists will also exert their human judgment and oversight in ways that make GPT-4 most productive, too.

SOCIAL MEDIA

AT ONLY TWENTY-FOUR, JIMMY DONALDSON, aka MrBeast, has created a collection of YouTube channels that collectively boast 221 million subscribers and more than 35 billion total views. Clearly he knows a thing or two about how to scale.

One of the things that most stands out to me about MrBeast is how good he and his team are at creating titles for his videos that tell you exactly what you're going to see in a way that makes you want to watch it.

"Would You Sit in Snakes for $10,000?"

"1000 Blind People See for the First Time."

"Can 50,000 Magnets Catch a Cannon Ball?"

There's no question what any of those videos are about, and no question that I want to watch them. I mean, aren't you wondering right now if 50,000 magnets *can* catch a cannonball? The content is the marketing.

Perhaps not surprisingly, then, one of the first things I did when I started thinking about GPT-4's potential impact on social media was to spend an hour or so feeding GPT-4 various prompts to generate titles for potential MrBeast videos. While GPT-4 produced fairly generic responses much of the time, its extreme generativity means its success rate doesn't have to be high. Here's a few that I felt were its best responses:

> **Reid:** Create twenty-five titles for funny MrBeast videos that feature a Lamborghini versus something else.
>
> **GPT-4:** Lamborghini vs 10,000 Balloons: Can It Float?
>
> **Reid:** Create twenty-five titles for hilarious and creative MrBeast videos involving hot sauce.
>
> **GPT-4:** I Filled a Pool with Hot Sauce and Dared My Friends to Swim in It
>
> **Reid:** Create the headline for a MrBeast video if MrBeast were a radical Marxist.
>
> **GPT-4:** I Bought an Entire Factory and Gave It to the Workers
>
> **Reid:** Create twenty titles for wacky and inventive MrBeast videos that involve the world's largest 3D printer printing unusual things.
>
> **GPT-4:** I 3D Printed a Giant Ice Cream Cone and Ate It with a Forklift
>
> **Reid:** Create twenty titles for crazy MrBeast videos involving commercial space travel.
>
> **GPT-4:** I Hired Elon Musk to Be My Personal Space Guide

Since I'm not exactly in MrBeast's demo, I'm definitely not the best judge of GPT-4's performance here. But don't you want to see if 10,000 balloons can make a Lamborghini float? At the very least, GPT-4 performed well enough to make me wonder what MrBeast and his team might come up with if they tried to generate prompts with it, too.

If they ever do, they'll have a lot of company. Already, YouTube is filled with literally thousands of videos about ChatGPT. My favorites are the ones that directly engage ChatGPT. In one, an influencer who goes by the name Grackle gives ChatGPT a rave review[17] after trying out its recipe for cookie dough-stuffed cupcakes: "It's actually really good! What a little dream match made in heaven!"

In another, a physician named Doctor Mike quizzes ChatGPT on a range of medical subjects.[18] He is particularly impressed with ChatGPT's nuanced reply to a question involving ethics: "That was a really smart answer!"

Automation for the people

It doesn't surprise me that YouTube creators have greeted recent AI advances with enthusiasm. Social media has always been populated by upstarts and iconoclasts with often unorthodox ideas about where to push things next.

It's also a medium where AI has played a defining role for some time. Automated content-moderation algorithms help keep spam, hate speech, disinformation, and NSFHE* imagery at bay on most of the major platforms, enabling you to publish your own posts almost instantaneously, without need for comparatively slow oversight from human moderators. AI algorithms help tailor content and product recommendations to your own specific tastes.

Of course AI can create issues in social media, too. Algorithms designed to maximize user engagement can lead to filter bubbles and echo chambers, exposing users to narrower and more extreme kinds of content. Algorithms that create, say, auto-generated "memories" videos can cause real discomfort if

---

*   Not safe for human eyeballs.

the resulting content includes people or occasions you'd rather not be reminded of.

Importantly, with both the good and the bad, social media users haven't had much agency over how AI shapes their experiences. About the most they've been able to do is opt out of various uses, such as turning off personalized advertising or those memories videos. What they haven't had, until recently, are opportunities to use AI in the kind of opt-in, largely self-directed ways that tools like GPT-4 and DALL-E 2 enable.

This is a theme I've touched on throughout this travelog, but it's especially relevant in this chapter. From its inception, social media worked to recast broadcast media's monolithic and passive audiences as interactive, democratic communities, in which newly empowered participants could connect directly with each other. They could project their own voices broadly, with no editorial "gatekeeping" beyond a given platform's terms of service.

Even with the rise of recommendation algorithms, social media remains a medium where users have more chance to determine their own pathways and experiences than they do in the world of traditional media. It's a medium where they've come to expect a certain level of autonomy, and typically they look for new ways to expand it.

Social media content creators also wear a lot of hats, especially when starting out. A new YouTube creator is probably not only functioning as her channel's on-screen talent, but also its producer, director, writer, editor, publicist, etc.

The utility of AI is obvious in this context: it's a powerful way for creators to amplify their productive power. But it also presents a seeming paradox. Precisely because of social media's hands-on, do-it-yourself nature, authenticity is the medium's lodestar. Creators and consumers alike value immediacy, spontaneity, and an explicitly human touch.

So AI might, at first glance, seem like a tricky fit. But it's also true that the medium's signature artifact, the selfie, is as much a technological triumph as it is an aesthetic one. Thanks to the smartphone's superior form factor, snapshot portraiture requires much less manpower than it once did.

I believe AI will be an even more powerful instance of that dynamic.

Am I bot or not?

While authenticity may be social media's coin of the realm, a lot of counterfeiting goes on there, too. And I don't just mean aesthetically, like when an endless summer Instagram filter bathes the line between authenticity and artifice in an ambient golden glow. I mean potentially harmful forms of deception, like fake news stories, manipulated video, or that farmer from Iowa on Twitter who isn't really a farmer, or Iowan, or human.

Between the bots and the deepfakes, does it really make sense to add this kind of AI to the mix?

While I addressed this in the Journalism chapter, it makes sense to address it here too. After all, it's social media that has helped make disinformation so spreadable.

It's worth remembering that things didn't start out this way. In many of its earliest incarnations, social media actually helped bring transparency and veracity to the online world.

For example, when my co-founders and I launched LinkedIn twenty years ago, we were motivated largely by the fact that the divisions between "cyberspace" and "the real world" were rapidly collapsing. Instead of existing as a place that people "went to" under the cover of pseudonymous screen names, the internet had evolved into a place that people were using to facilitate their lives. They went there to buy things, and stay in touch with their families, and make plans with their real-world friends. In such a milieu, my co-founders and I realized, digital platforms built on real identity could be hugely beneficial to hundreds of millions of people.

In LinkedIn's case, of course, we focused on professional identity. To create trust on our platform, we positioned a user's identity in networks of affiliation. That way, you couldn't just craft a fictional persona out of thin air—other users effectively confirmed that you were who you said you were.

At Facebook, launched a year later, participation was initially limited to students with verified college email addresses. And while Facebook didn't *require* new users to upload photos of themselves, that's clearly the norm it was hoping to establish.

Through such approaches, social media helped real identity take root online in a meaningful way for the first time. And yet social media's emphasis on broad participation also left it vulnerable to various kinds of deception, some human-generated, some automated. As I've written elsewhere,[19] I believe most social media platforms underestimated how much governance online communities would require, especially as they scaled to hundreds of millions of users or more.

Over time, most social media platforms have substantially increased their governance efforts, often through the use of AI tools that play a central role in combatting disinformation, fraud, and other kinds of deception. But it's an ongoing battle. Facebook, for example, now regularly takes down more than one billion fake accounts[20] per quarter.

So even if we tried to prohibit broad democratic access to AI tools, fraud and deception challenges would persist.

To me, the most effective and most equitable path forward involves thinking about new approaches rather than hard-to-enforce bans. As I described in the Journalism chapter, I think "flooding the zone with truth" is one key way to combat disinformation.

On a similar note, I think we'll start to see social media participants, and especially social media creators, develop and implement new ways to verify their status as human beings. Platforms themselves will likely participate in this process, continuing and expanding on their early efforts to establish real identity.

How exactly this will play out I'm not sure. It just strikes me that, as the logical consequence of living in a world where AI tools can convincingly simulate human expression, actual humans will seek ways to convey that they are corporeal beings. In short, they will flood the zone with their humanity.

If you're thinking that maybe this sounds like a lot of trouble to go through just to enable a world where hustle bros[21] fill the web with spam and SEO content, it's important to always keep two key facts in mind.

The first is that AI tools capable of communicating in human-like ways are by no means inherently deceptive. It's all about intention. A customer-service chatbot that clearly conveys its status as a non-human entity is in fact behaving in an extremely authentic manner.

The second is that while AI tools can potentially cause confusion when used deceptively, they will also create great value when used transparently and straightforwardly.

Everyone has entered the chat

It took less than a week for ChatGPT to show how much people actually *like* conversing with chatbots when those chatbots possess human-like fluency instead of a narrow range of canned responses. So imagine when every airline, shipping service, online retailer, and government agency in the world begins to deploy chatbots as capable of answering your questions as GPT-4.

Now, to extend this further—and to bring this line of thought back to social media—imagine having extended conversations with chatbot versions of MrBeast, Michelle Obama, Benjamin Franklin, Marge Simpson, the world's best high school math tutor, an expert on B2B marketing, etc.

I'm not saying this world is coming next month, or even next year. But I do think that LLM chatbots of this type will eventually join the ranks of books, podcasts, instructional videos, music albums, and other media formats that individuals use to syndicate their thoughts, values, personality, and creativity across time and space.

Of course, this isn't an endeavor without risk, at least as long as LLMs continue to produce hallucinations and other unintended consequences at not-insignificant rates. So I don't expect someone of Michelle Obama's stature to lead the charge.

Instead, it will likely be people who are willing to take on some risk in return for a shot at pioneering a field where early adopters could reap outsized rewards. My guess is that most will emerge from the ranks of social media.

In part, this is because a chatbot like this could help address a common social media challenge. To show you what I mean, let's imagine a fictional YouTube creator I'll call Codysseus. Codysseus is a twenty-five-year-old software developer who travels around North America in his van conversion, accompanied by his pet cat Clickbait.

When Codysseus arrives at a new destination, he usually ends up staying in the most unique Airbnb he can find. When no rentals are available, he just stays in his van. Since remote computer work is not particularly cinematic, Codysseus also spends a fair amount of time exploring his latest habitat in search of material he can use in the weekly episodes he posts to YouTube. Sometimes he takes odd jobs in the hope of creating more fodder for his channel. Sometimes he gives seminars to the locals on how to approximate his digital nomad life.

In the early days of his channel, Codysseus was vigilant about answering every viewer comment within twenty-four hours. He quickly learned that maintaining this high level of responsiveness turned one-time viewers into repeat viewers, and repeat viewers into subscribers. But now that he has 150,000 subscribers and a new video can get upwards of 1000 comments, he has to leave more and more questions unanswered.

Not surprisingly, given his work as a software developer, Codysseus starts thinking about how AI could help him out. Initially, his focus is on how he might automate replies to the comments his viewers leave him on YouTube. At a certain point, however, he realizes that creating a full-blown chatbot of himself would be even more compelling. It would give his fans an ongoing, in-depth way to interact with him. It might become a source of real insights about what his fans like best about his content and his persona. It could even generate revenues.

How possible is it for someone like Codysseus to create their own LLM chatbot now?

Here's what GPT-4 replied when I put the question to it:

> **Reid:** Assume that GPT-4 is publicly accessible, afford-able, and scalable, and that it has significantly improved on GPT-3's capabilities in terms of generalization, coher-ence, and diversity. If all this is true, would a YouTube creator named Codysseus, with a catalog of transcripts from more than a hundred fifteen-minute episodes, plus 20,000+ words of blog archives, plus 2000+ replies to viewer comments, plus 500+ Reddit posts be able to use this data to effectively create a fine-tuned version of GPT-4 that approximates his speech patterns, sensibil-ities and values, sense of humor, guiding interests and aspirations, and generally conveys his personality?

> **GPT-4:** Possible answer: Yes, a YouTube creator named Codysseus would likely be able to use this data to effec-tively create a fine-tuned version of GPT-4 that approx-imates his speech patterns, sensibilities and values, sense of humor, guiding interests and aspirations, and generally conveys his personality. Assuming that GPT-4 is publicly accessible, affordable, and scalable, and that it has significantly improved on GPT-3's capabilities,

Codysseus could leverage the large and diverse corpus of his own written and spoken content to train a custom model that captures his unique voice and style. He could also use additional data sources, such as feedback from his audience, social media interactions, and relevant topics and trends, to further refine and update his model. By fine-tuning GPT-4 on his own data, Codysseus could potentially generate new content that is consistent, coherent, and creative, and that reflects his personality and preferences. He could also use his model to interact with his fans, answer questions, and provide commentary on various issues. However, Codysseus would also need to be careful and ethical in using his model, and ensure that he discloses and acknowledges the use of GPT-4 to his viewers and followers. He would also need to monitor and evaluate his model's outputs, and correct any errors, biases, or inaccuracies that might arise. Moreover, he would need to respect the intellectual property and privacy rights of others, and avoid plagiarizing or misrepresenting any sources or information. Finally, he would need to maintain his own authenticity and integrity, and not rely solely on his model to express himself or engage with his community.

In short, it's quite possible that someone like Codysseus could do this already.

It would take him some time and effort to arrange all his source data—the YouTube transcripts, blog posts, etc.—into the format that the fine-tuning process requires. At that point, though, he'd be able to use the resources OpenAI provides at extremely low cost. (In Codysseus' hypothetical case, OpenAI would probably charge him around $30 for its fine-tuning process.)

As usual, GPT-4 emphasizes the same themes I've been emphasizing throughout this travelog: the value of transparency, ongoing human oversight, and complementarity. If Codysseus were open about his chatbot usage, and presented this digital entity transparently as an extension of himself (instead of trying to pass it off as the real him), his opportunities would increase accordingly.

He might, for example, ultimately create multiple fine-tuned models of himself. One might focus primarily on coding instruction. Another might offer advice specifically on digital nomadism. Perhaps he'd even create a chatbot—make that a *catbot*—to embody Clickbait.

Some of these iterations might be available only to paying subscribers. Others might be underwritten by sponsors whose products and services the chatbot occasionally mentions. All would potentially increase the value of the human Codysseus as an advertising spokesperson, business consultant, or events speaker, to name just a few possibilities, just as books, podcasts, and other media artifacts already perform this function.

Social media AI: the next generations

When YouTube launched in 2005, no one was quick to predict that it would evolve into one of the world's greatest educational and reference resources. No one foresaw that it was about to turn cats into millionaires. No one was anticipating the rapid growth and mainstreaming of content genres like reaction videos, makeup videos, unboxing videos, ASMR videos, and so many others.

Instead, thousands of innovative creators equipped with powerful new tools and capabilities simply started exploring their crazy ideas and passions—and sometimes magic happened.

This cycle is about to repeat itself, this time with AI. So the chatbot example I've focused on in this chapter is just one of countless possible paths forward. Those who truly crack the codes here will likely do so with ideas and approaches no one has yet to imagine. For them, an incredible future of creative fulfillment and high impact awaits.

TRANSFORMATION OF WORK

WHEN I GRADUATED FROM COLLEGE IN 1990, jobs like "web designer," "SEO strategist," and "data scientist" didn't exist.

When my co-founders and I launched LinkedIn thirteen years later in 2003, none of our users had jobs like "social media manager," "TikTok influencer," or "virtual reality architect."

With GPT-4 and other forms of AI, we're going to see similar impacts on industry trends, overall work patterns, and career paths. The companies, professions, and individuals who figure out how to incorporate these new tools into their workflows in the most innovative and productive ways will fare best. The ones that don't adapt in strategic ways will struggle to maintain their relevance and competitiveness in a changing marketplace.

In my opinion, ignoring AI is like ignoring blogging in the late 1990s, or social media circa 2004, or mobile in 2007. Very quickly, some degree of facility with these tools will be increasingly essential for all professionals, a primary driver for new opportunities and new jobs. Developing skills and competencies in it now will yield benefits for years to come.

It's also true that the changes AI will bring will have negative impacts as well as positive ones. Previous technology revolutions disrupted specific subgroups, like the craftsmen whose production was replaced by factories—or, more recently, factory workers who lost their jobs to increased automation.

Now, knowledge workers are also facing these challenges. While I strongly believe that these new AI tools will create new jobs and new industries, along with great economic benefits and other quality-of-life gains, they will also eliminate some jobs, both blue- and white-collar.

In light of this reality, policy makers and business leaders can take a number of steps to help facilitate this transition. This includes investing in training and retraining programs to ensure that workers are equipped with the necessary skills to take on new roles. It means creating safety nets for workers affected by automation.

To navigate this moment most effectively, though, we must also do so with an adaptive, forward-looking perspective. In my mind, that means embracing AI in the same spirit that we once embraced the Model T and the Apple II. In the past, it has always been breakthrough technologies that have created the jobs of the future—and I expect it to be no different this time.

The transformation of careers

Back in 2012, Ben Casnocha and I published *The Start-up of You*, our book on modern career management. We felt that far too often, the societal conversation about careers focused on how changes were making it difficult to follow the old model of joining a company and working your way up the ladder until you retired with a gold watch and a pension. People were clinging to old lessons that no longer applied, and mourning their loss.

A far better approach, we thought, was to adapt to the future by learning new lessons that would apply in a world with much greater job mobility.

A decade later, we published the revised and updated edition of *The Startup of You* (note the dropping of the hyphen) to incorporate some of the major shifts that had occurred, from the massive increase in gig work to the effects of the COVID-19 pandemic and the move to hybrid remote and in-person workplaces.

We may well have to write a third edition to cover the rise of AI, and if so, we probably won't wait until 2032 to publish it. (Who knows? By the time the third edition comes out, GPT-4 may be a full co-author.)

Yes, changes may make it harder to follow the old career models, but a much more productive path is to look forward to how changes enable new opportunities. People need to ask themselves, "What could possibly go right?"

Let's explore some of the possible themes here.

Reid: How might individual professionals use AI to help them implement the key career management concepts and recommendations found in the book *The Startup of You* by Reid Hoffman and Ben Casnocha? Please write the answer in the form of a bulleted list.

GPT-4:

- Analyze data about an individual's skills, experiences, and interests to identify career opportunities that align with their goals.

- Suggest networking strategies and develop personalized strategies for marketing their personal brand.

- Recommend mentors and advisors that could help the individual advance their career.

- Identify risks and potential failure points before taking action, allowing the individual to make better decisions.

I can see how tools like GPT-4 could help identify career opportunities, recommend mentors and advisors (though of course convincing the targets so identified to become a mentor or advisor is its own challenge), and identify potential risks and failure points. I can even see it suggesting specific networking strategies. But how would it develop a personalized strategy, for a personal brand, when such a thing is necessarily, well, personal?

Reid: Please develop a set of personalized strategies for author and venture capitalist Ben Casnocha to market his personal brand. This should include a summary of Ben's current personal brand, how that brand could be refined and improved, and a set of specific actions that Ben should take to market his personal brand.

GPT-4: Ben Casnocha's current personal brand is that of an accomplished author, venture capitalist, and technology enthusiast. He is well-known for his books *The Alliance, The Start-up of You*, and *Bold*, and is a partner at the venture capital firm Village Global. His brand could be improved by increasing his visibility in the technology industry and highlighting his specific expertise. To market his personal brand, Ben should consider the following strategies:

- Speak at technology conferences and industry events to increase his visibility and establish himself as a thought leader in the industry.

- Leverage his social media presence to promote his books, articles, and speaking engagements.

- Connect with top technology influencers to expand his network and build relationships with key industry players.

- Launch a podcast or web series to engage with a larger audience and share his knowledge and insights.

- Publish articles in industry magazines and websites to demonstrate his expertise and showcase his work.

- Participate in entrepreneurship competitions and hackathons to increase his visibility and network with other entrepreneurs.

- Create a personal website to showcase his work and provide an online hub for his audience.

OK. First of all, there's a factual error. *Bold* is actually by Peter Diamandis and Steven Kotler; Ben's first book was *My Start-up Life*.

More importantly, GPT-4's recommendations are as generic as can be. There is nothing personalized about any of that advice.

Let's try asking a more general question.

Reid: What are some of the most impactful ways that a young professional can use AI to help her manage her career, accelerate her career progression, and find more meaningful and fulfilling work in a future where the broad adoption of AI technologies and tools has already transformed how humans work?

GPT-4:

- Automated career planning: AI can help you make informed decisions about your career and provide personalized guidance for career development. You can use AI algorithms to create a personalized plan for career progression and identify key steps to success.

- Automated skills assessment: AI can help you assess your current skills and identify new skills that you need to acquire in order to advance your career. This can enable you to stay updated with the latest industry trends and develop the skills required to stay competitive.

- Automated job matching: AI can help you find the right job opportunities that best match your skills and experience. By leveraging AI algorithms, you can get personalized recommendations for job postings that are most suitable for you.

- Automated resume optimization: AI can help you create the perfect resume that highlights your skills and experience. You can use AI algorithms to identify the best combination of words and phrases to make your resume stand out.

- Automated job interview preparation: AI can help you prepare for job interviews by providing personalized guidance. You can use AI algorithms to analyze the job description and identify the questions that you will likely be asked during the interview.

It feels like GPT-4 is having the terms "automated" and "algorithms" do a lot of work there. Nonetheless, the advice seems sound.

My personal "human intelligence" take is that AI can serve as your co-captain as you steer the ship of your career. The core insight of *The Startup of You* is that your career is like a startup, and you are its CEO. Being a startup CEO is a lonely and stressful job, full of uncertainty and paralyzing dilemmas. One way to make the job a bit more manageable is to build a personal board of advisors who can help and support you, but even that approach has its limitations.

Your board members, being human, won't always be available to talk. GPT-4 and other such AI tools can serve as an AI advisor, helping you analyze any situation and generate options, and will do so on-demand, at any time, in a matter of seconds. GPT-4's suggestions won't always be immediately helpful, but they will provide something to react to and build on, which is better than being stuck with a blank page.

The transformation of management

Shortly after Ben and I published *The Startup of You*, we realized that creating a new framework for how individual professionals should approach their careers also created the need for a new framework for how employers and managers should work with these newly empowered and entrepreneurial professionals.

So we asked our old friend Chris Yeh to explore those implications with us in a second book, *The Alliance*.

That book's thesis is that organizations and managers are using outdated metaphors to think about the employment relationship. Many CEOs want to think of their employees as family, but family implies a permanent and virtually unbreakable relationship that just isn't practical in the modern workplace. Other leaders go too far in the other direction, conceiving of their employees as purely free agents, making it nearly impossible to build trust, loyalty, and long-term value.

The better metaphor, we assert, is to think of employees as allies—independent entities who come together to pursue an important shared mission, complete with an explicit agreement about what constitutes success and how success makes the business stronger and accelerates the employee's career progression.

Now let's bring in AI.

Reid: How might organizations and managers use AI to help them implement the key management concepts and recommendations found in the 2014 book *The Alliance* by Reid Hoffman, Ben Casnocha, and Chris Yeh? Please make sure you write about building an alliance between employee and employer, defining a specific "tour of duty" for the employee, which lays out a specific mission that benefits both employer and employee, and how employers can establish and leverage a corporate alumni network to stay in touch with former employees. Please write the answer in the form of a bulleted list.

GPT-4:

- AI can be used to help build strong relationships between employers and employees by providing personalized, real-time feedback on performance and job satisfaction.

- AI can help organizations define specific "tours of duty" for employees, which lay out the specific mission that both employer and employee can benefit from.

- AI can help employers establish and leverage corporate alumni networks to stay in touch with former employees and understand their motivations, skills, and experiences.

- AI can help organizations create a culture of trust and collaboration by providing employees with tailored advice and assistance as needed.

- AI can help organizations create a culture of transparency and openness by providing employees with access to up-to-date information about the company's performance and goals.

- AI can help organizations create a culture of learning and continuous improvement by providing employees with personalized training and development opportunities.

- AI can help organizations establish a system of feedback and reward employees for their achievements, by providing employees with timely feedback and recognition.

I like a lot of the ideas here, even if some lack an obvious connection with *The Alliance* (for example, our book doesn't discuss "cultures of learning" or reward systems). The modern workplace is so busy that managers have fewer and fewer opportunities to provide timely feedback to their direct reports, and vice versa. The rise of remote and hybrid workplaces only exacerbates the problem. I'm excited that AI could help improve the employee experience by offering feedback and development when they want it, rather than when their schedule happens to line up with their manager's.

Diving deeper . . .

Reid: What are some of the ways AI can be used to help build strong relationships between employers and employees by providing personalized, real-time feedback on performance and job satisfaction?

GPT-4: AI can be used to . . .

- Provide employees with personalized advice and assistance on specific tasks or projects.

- Identify areas of improvement and provide tailored guidance to employees on how to improve their performance.

- Provide employees with up-to-date feedback on their performance and job satisfaction.

- Provide employees with timely recognition for their achievements.

- Provide employees with tailored training and development opportunities.

- Analyze employee sentiment and provide employers with an understanding of employee engagement and job satisfaction.

What strikes me is how we ask managers to do all of these things today with little to no support from technology (with the possible exception of sentiment analysis). I'm still not sure how AI will do all of these things, but if it does, it will be a huge boon to managers.

Reid: What are some of the ways AI can help organizations define specific "tours of duty" for employees, which lay out a specific mission that both employer and employee can benefit from?

GPT-4: AI can be used to . . .

- Develop specific job descriptions and tasks, tailored to the employee's skills and interests.

- Identify potential opportunities for employees to progress and develop their skills.

- Provide employees with personalized guidance and advice on how to achieve their goals.

- Analyze employee performance and suggest areas to focus on and improve.

- Provide employees with tailored goal-setting and progress tracking tools.

- Provide employees with individualized feedback and recognition for their achievements.

In *The Startup of You* and *The Alliance,* we lay out the case that individuals need to take control of their own career journey. This is undoubtedly true, but remains daunting. The promise of AI is that it will help people with these meta tasks that exist in parallel with explicit work assignments in order to help every employee, not just the most self-motivated and disciplined, optimize their work performance and career progression.

Reid: Write a story of around 400 words about a manager and employee in the year 2035 using AI to work together to define a tour of duty for that employee, and leveraging AI to help that employee achieve greater productivity and accelerated career development. Illustrate the benefits to the company, the manager, and the employee of this approach.

GPT-4: It was the year 2035, and the world of work had changed drastically. AI-powered automation and artificial intelligence had transformed the way businesses operated, leading to increased efficiency and productivity.

Mark was the manager of a small tech company, and he was tasked with finding ways to increase the company's output and profits. He knew he needed to find a way to motivate and engage his employees, but he was unsure of how to do so.

One day, he was discussing the issue with a colleague when he was struck with an idea: what if he could use AI to create a "tour of duty" for each employee? He could use AI to define specific goals and tasks for each employee, as well as provide personalized guidance and feedback on their progress.

Mark quickly set to work creating the system. He used AI to define the tasks for each employee and provide tailored feedback. He also used AI to analyze employee sentiment and provide employees with timely recognition for their achievements.

The results were immediate and impressive. Productivity skyrocketed as employees felt more motivated and engaged in their work. Mark also noticed that the morale of his team had improved, as they felt more empowered and valued.

But the greatest benefit was to the company. With AI-powered automation and guidance, Mark was able to create a highly efficient and productive team. Profits soared, and the company's reputation quickly spread.

Mark had found the perfect solution to his problem. With AI-powered tours of duty, he had managed to create an engaged and motivated workforce, while also increasing the company's output and profits.

Love it!

Now let's take a closer look at how some specific professions that are often identified as being endangered by AI might fare in the future.

Sales

Daniel Pink once wrote a #1 *New York Times* bestseller titled *To Sell Is Human: The Surprising Truth About Moving Others*. It's hard to picture a computer as a salesperson. How would an AI build rapport by pointing out that you went to the same school as it, or sharing funny stories about raising its kids?

At the same time, I can easily imagine how tools like GPT-4 could amplify human salespeople. Great salespeople take the time to deeply understand their potential buyer and, ideally, can customize a sales presentation to address their specific needs and make it easy for the buyer to visualize success.

Let's see what GPT-4 thinks.

> **Reid:** How will the adoption of AI tools transform the profession of sales? Please address the key activities in the sales funnel, such as prospecting, qualifying leads, presenting to the buyer, closing the deal, and helping customers succeed.

> **GPT-4:** The adoption of AI tools has the potential to transform the profession of sales in a number of ways.

> Firstly, AI-driven automation of sales processes can dramatically increase sales productivity and efficiency. AI-powered tools can help sales reps easily identify potential leads, qualify them, and prioritize them based on the likelihood of successful sales outcomes. AI-driven automation can also help sales reps quickly create compelling presentations tailored to their customer's needs and preferences.

> In addition, AI-driven customer insights can be used to better understand customer behaviors, needs, and preferences to inform better sales strategies and tactics. AI-driven customer insights can also be used to personalize sales pitches and better target customer segments.

> Finally, AI-driven tools can help sales reps close deals more quickly and effectively by providing timely insights into customer sentiment and helping sales reps identify the best time to reach out and close the deal. AI-driven tools can also help sales reps provide post-sale customer success by helping them anticipate customer needs and proactively reach out with helpful solutions.

This resonates with my own experience. Analyzing and qualifying leads, understanding customer behavior and needs, personalizing sales pitches, staying on top of customer sentiment, and proactively reaching out to customers after a deal is closed are time-consuming. That's why only the best, most dedicated human sales professionals do a good job with them.

For example, if I wanted to maximize my chances of making a sale, I would look up my buyer on LinkedIn and analyze her profile. I would also research her non-business social media posts to understand her likes, dislikes, and passions. I would tailor my sales presentation to reflect past projects she's worked on, or might work on in the future. (One of my AI investments, Tome, is already making it easier to create great presentations!) I would watch the news for events at her company that might affect her buying decision. And, post-sale, I'd monitor how she was using my product so I could suggest ways to add more value and solve other problems.

Of course, doing this for every customer is incredibly time-consuming.

Too many human salespeople prefer to simply "churn and burn," calling sales "a numbers game." This is especially true for startups, where the product and market may not be mature enough for a simple, repeatable sales process.

AI-amplified sales might offer the best of both worlds by doing much of the hard work that many human sales professionals skip, allowing the humans to focus instead on what AI can't do, like building relationships with the buyer and reading emotional cues during sales calls.

So far, all good for salespeople. But is there a downside?

Reid: How will the adoption of AI tools negatively impact the careers of human sales professionals?

GPT-4: The adoption of AI tools is likely to have a significant and direct negative impact on the careers of human sales professionals. AI-driven automation of sales processes will reduce the need for human sales reps to perform certain tasks, such as prospecting and qualifying leads, creating presentations, and closing deals. AI-driven automation is likely to lead to a reduction in the number of human sales reps required to perform these tasks.

In addition, AI-driven customer insights will reduce the need for human sales reps to analyze customer data and develop customer segmentation strategies. AI-driven customer insights are likely to lead to fewer opportunities for human sales reps to use their insights and expertise to inform sales strategies.

Finally, AI-driven tools may make it easier for customers to find solutions to their needs without the help of a human sales rep. This could reduce the need for human sales reps to provide customer service and lead to fewer opportunities for sales reps to interact with customers and make sales.

GPT-4 sure isn't mincing words here. Today, many in enterprise sales get their start as a Business Development Representative (BDR). These early-career professionals "dial for dollars" with outbound calls, emails, and yes, LinkedIn messages. While the work is tedious, it is still work, and those who excel at it often win promotion to full-fledged sales positions.

AI will make human BDRs more effective by providing them with personalized information on the prospects they call—but this increased productivity will likely decrease employment, because buyers only have so much money. This result is still better for society as a whole, since bad sales calls are a waste of every participant's time, but it will reduce the overall level of employment in the profession.

I believe that the future will see the sales profession shrink as a whole. At the same time, the productivity of individual sales professionals will increase, and likely their compensation as well. And the AI-driven increased quality of selling means that companies that aggressively adopt these tools will beat any competitors that don't.

Law

I have personal reasons for my interest in how AI will affect lawyers. Both my parents practiced law, and from a young age, I've had direct personal experience with the profession. I'm powerfully curious how AI might change it.

> **Reid:** What are some ways in which AI may be better suited to handle some legal tasks than human attorneys? Which legal tasks are the most easily automated using AI? What are the legal tasks where AIs will likely outperform human lawyers?

> **GPT-4:** AI is better suited for tasks that require large amounts of data and information to be analyzed and organized quickly and accurately. AI can quickly search through large data sets and identify patterns and trends, as well as draw conclusions from the data. AI can also automate low-level legal tasks, such as document review and contract review, which can be tedious and time consuming for human lawyers. AI may also be able to predict the outcome of a legal case, given certain facts and evidence. AI is also better suited for tasks that require precise, technical analysis, such as patent searches or financial analysis.

I can see how AI could equal or exceed the work of human clerks and paralegals for conducting patent searches, digging through discovery data, or searching for red flags in long, boring contracts. Leveraging AI might also be a good first step before bringing in an (expensive) outside expert, or to make a lawyer's usage of such an expert more effective.

Now let's look at the positive case.

Reid: How might the adoption of AI in the practice of law positively impact the career prospects of current attorneys? What steps might those lawyers take to enhance their careers by using AI in their work?

GPT-4: The adoption of AI in the practice of law could potentially lead to increased job opportunities for lawyers, as AI technology can automate certain routine tasks, freeing up lawyers' time to focus on more complex and challenging areas of law. Lawyers can also use AI to enhance their understanding of the law by taking advantage of AI's ability to quickly search through large amounts of data and information. Lawyers can also utilize AI to better understand the legal implications of certain cases and to develop creative solutions to legal issues. Lawyers can stay ahead of the curve by continuously learning about the latest advancements in AI technology and how it can be applied to the practice of law.

In my personal experience, the actual practice of law is more boring, tedious, and detail-obsessed than the typical television program or movie makes it seem. There's a lot less delivering eloquent speeches to a jury, and a lot more reading thousands of pages of poorly written documents. AI would be terrible at the former, but is very good at the latter.

While AI certainly has the potential to disrupt the way we currently handle low-level legal work, it also has the potential to improve the happiness of an often-unhappy profession. I'm not sure any human attorneys ever enjoy reading thousands of nearly identical contracts, however well they are paid!

Management consulting

The tech industry is notoriously skeptical of management consulting, but having worked with many smart, high-integrity professionals at firms like McKinsey, I believe management consultants can play an important role in business (albeit rarely at startups with fewer than one hundred employees.)

Management consultants are often called upon to draw conclusions from large amounts of data, to benchmark and share best practices, and to create plans for starting and growing new business units. A lot of these tasks feel like they might be well-suited to AI.

Let's test that intuition.

> **Reid:** What are some of the ways that AI could be used to perform the important functions of management consulting?

> **GPT-4:**

> - AI could be used to help identify opportunities for improvement and cost savings in businesses by analyzing data sets and recommending strategies and tactics.

> - AI could be used to help with forecasting and predictive analysis to better anticipate market trends, customer behavior, and other economic conditions.

> - AI could be used to generate insights from customer feedback and employee surveys, allowing for more targeted and effective management consulting activities.

- AI could be used to collect and analyze data on competitors and industry trends, helping to identify areas for improvement and growth.

- AI could be used to automate and speed up the process of crafting and implementing strategies, allowing for more efficient and effective management consulting.

GPT-4 puts a lot of emphasis on analyzing data and drawing conclusions here, which seems logical—that's what Bain and BCG and their compadres do. But if AI is doing so much analysis, what happens to the human consultants?

Reid: How might the adoption of AI within the management consulting industry negatively impact the career prospects of current consultants? Provide examples of how these changes will affect early-career analysts and associates, mid-career engagement managers, and high-level executives such as McKinsey partners.

GPT-4: The adoption of AI within the management consulting industry could have a negative impact on the career prospects of current consultants. Early-career analysts and associates may be the most affected, as AI can automate many of the tasks they are responsible for, such as research, data analysis, and report writing. As AI systems become more sophisticated, these roles may become redundant, leading to a decrease in job opportunities for these individuals.

Mid-career engagement managers may also be affected by the adoption of AI. AI systems may be able to automate the processes of creating and implementing strategies, making engagement managers' roles less necessary. They may also be replaced by AI systems in their role of providing insights and advice to clients, as AI systems become more capable of performing these tasks.

> Even high-level executives such as McKinsey partners may be affected by the adoption of AI. AI systems may be able to automate decision-making and strategy implementation, making the role of the partner less essential. Additionally, AI systems may be able to generate insights and advice for clients, reducing the need for partners to provide their own expertise.

These answers seem reasonable. A lot of the "grunt work" that the analysts and associates perform—which includes a lot of web searching and drafting PowerPoint slides—could be performed by tools such as GPT-4 and Tome. And, to the extent that a client hires a management consulting firm to provide the conventional wisdom on a topic, why not turn to AI to conduct a truly comprehensive review of the source data?

Management consultants who are unable to add value beyond these standardized activities will suffer. A firm can't pay young analysts and associates to "turn the crank" and then charge the client ten times their salary for their output. But management consultants who can take the time that AI frees up and focus instead on generating more unconventional insights could devote more of their time to this high-value activity and deliver even better service to their clients with the help of AI.

One potential issue is, if management consulting firms aren't hiring armies of bright young university and B-school graduates to perform the basic tasks of management consulting, how will the next generation of partners learn their craft? Let's see if AI can solve the problem.

> **Reid:** In the future, how might management consulting firms use AI to help train and upskill entry-level analysts and associates, if those young consultants aren't get-

ting the opportunity to learn their craft by performing the research and analysis tasks that have been taken over by AI?

GPT-4: Management consulting firms may use AI to help train and upskill entry-level analysts and associates in the future. AI systems can be used to simulate real-world scenarios and provide virtual coaching to young consultants, helping them to hone their skills and gain experience with the use of AI. Additionally, AI systems can be used to provide personalized learning plans for young consultants, helping them to focus on the areas where they need the most development.

Firms may also use AI to provide virtual mentorship programs for entry-level analysts and associates. AI systems can be used to provide personalized advice and guidance to young consultants, helping them to gain the skills and knowledge they need to succeed in their roles. Additionally, firms may use AI to facilitate the exchange of knowledge and insights between experienced consultants and entry-level analysts and associates, helping the young consultants to learn from their more experienced colleagues.

I like the concept of using AI-powered simulations to help train the human professionals of the future. Many young professionals complain about not getting enough opportunities to learn and the lack of mentorship. It may take some refinement, but perhaps AI can help solve these all-too-common issues.

As I reach this chapter's end, it occurs to me that I can perhaps save myself some work right now. Let's bring things to a conclusion with GPT-4's help.

Reid: Please write a 200-word conclusion to the [preceding] essay.

GPT-4:

A common theme throughout this essay is that AI will likely disrupt some professions more than others, but that the potential for positive change is immense. In some cases, such as with sales, AI will likely lead to a reduction in the overall number of jobs, but will also enable the remaining professionals to become more productive and effective. In other cases, such as with law, AI may lead to an overall improvement in the happiness and satisfaction of the profession.

While it is important to be aware of the ways in which AI may disrupt traditional career paths, it is also important to remember that AI can create new opportunities for growth and advancement. As we move into a future where AI tools are a core part of normal work processes, it is essential for professionals to take advantage of the opportunities that AI presents in order to achieve greater productivity and more meaningful work.

GPT-4 IN MY OWN WORK

IN THE SAME WAY I EXPECT GPT-4 and similar technologies to transform the world of work, I also expect them to transform the way *I* work. I've had the opportunity to experiment with GPT-4 for a few months, and while I know I'm still on the steep part of my learning curve, I believe I have enough experience to offer some advice on how to use these tools.

When transformational technologies appear, most people are tempted to plug them in as a substitute for an existing technology or technique. This seems sensible, since it minimizes the time and effort needed to start using the new tech, but this approach is actually a trap: seldom is the new technology an exact analogue for what came before.

When the internet first appeared, pioneering services like Yahoo! resembled online phone books. Directories were how we found things, so the seemingly logical first step was to create an online directory. We discovered over time that the better approach was to create a new tool: the search engine.

We're still at the online-phone-book stage of LLMs. It's unlikely to be a direct replacement for search engines across many of their use cases, but it will offer people new ways to gather relevant and useful information.

Here are three key principles I've found useful in my own attempts to use GPT-4 in my work.

Principle 1: Treat GPT-4 like an undergrad research assistant, not an omniscient oracle.

If you've ever worked with an undergraduate research assistant (or if you were one in college), you know that a helper like that is both powerful and limited in specific ways.

In some ways, GPT-4 far exceeds any human research assistant: it has access to an incredibly broad base of knowledge, it is blindingly fast, and it's available whenever you need it (as opposed to needing to study for midterms).

It also has many of the other drawbacks of a human research assistant: it's not an expert, its grasp of any particular subject is fairly shallow, and it gets things wrong. In fact, when it's wrong, it's worse than a human research assistant, since a human will often have the good sense to warn you when he or she isn't certain about the quality of their output.

Despite these drawbacks, the power of giving everyone access to nearly instantaneous, on-demand research help is truly remarkable. Just make sure you cross-check results with deeper sources and actual human experts.

Principle 2: Think of yourself as a director, not a carpenter.

When we work with tools, we are trained to think of them as an extension of us. A carpenter swings a hammer and gets one step closer to completing a house. He or she knows what the hammer will do each time it swings, and works accordingly.

This metaphor breaks down when it comes to tools like GPT-4. Rather than manipulating a physical tool to generate a predictable and planned result, using GPT-4 is like directing a scene from a movie.

As the director, you're working with an actor to elicit the best performance. You're not telling them, "Bend your neck fifteen degrees, and then after 2.5 seconds, look at the person across from you." Instead, you're asking them to make the audience feel a certain way: "Convince us you're in love."

GPT-4 isn't a human actor, but the process of directing it is similar. You have to coax out your desired result, and you may need to try many variations on a prompt in the same way a director might need to film multiple takes of the same scene. It's ultimately a collaborative process.

Principle 3: Just try it!

In most of our work, we're taught to plan in advance and avoid making mistakes. That's because implementing a plan is costly in terms of time and other resources—there's a reason a carpenter's adage is to measure twice and cut once.

But what if implementing a plan was cheaper and faster than thinking about it?

That's the confounding paradox of GPT-4 and LLMs. In far less time than it takes to debate a plan, GPT-4 can simply generate a complete response for you to review. If you don't like the response, you can throw it away and generate another one, or you might just generate three variations to give you more potential choices.

For example, I've already adopted the practice of trying out some simple prompts any time I have a significant piece of work in front of me.

Like sitting down to write this chapter.

Reid: What are some of the ways that investor, author, and philanthropist Reid Hoffman might use LLMs to be faster, more efficient, and more effective at his work?

GPT-4:

- Automated research: LLMs can be used to search for and find relevant information quickly and accurately. Hoffman could use this technology to quickly locate research and data that would be useful for his investments and philanthropic efforts.

- Automated content creation: LLMs can be used to create content such as articles and reports, saving Hoffman time and effort on research and writing.

- Automated analysis: LLMs can be used to analyze large amounts of data quickly and accurately, allowing Hoffman to make better and faster decisions.

- Automated communication: LLMs can be used to automate communication tasks such as answering emails and scheduling meetings, freeing up Hoffman's time for more important tasks.

- Automated investment decisions: LLMs can be used to make investment decisions based on complex data and algorithms, allowing Hoffman to make more informed decisions quickly.

As usual, I think GPT-4 provides some instant food for thought.

Research and analysis is definitely a good use of GPT-4, as it literally knows most of the internet circa 2021. Its knowledge is far more comprehensive than any human's, and future tools will likely be even more comprehensive.

Automated content creation is interesting as a way of creating instant first drafts, but I'm skeptical of claims that it can be used without human intervention for important writing—at least for my work. I would want to review and refine any articles or reports it produced, though this could still accelerate my throughput considerably.

I'm a bit more skeptical about the remaining suggestions, like automating my communications. People email me looking for decisions and introductions, and I'm not quite ready to let the AI take over those functions just yet.

As for making investment decisions, I think AI could help me make more informed investment decisions quickly by prompting thoughts and helping me consider all the potential data points, but labeling this process an "automated investment decision" seems like a stretch.

Despite these minor objections, GPT-4 helped me tackle this chapter by generating a reasonable taxonomy of my work, with pointers to where I might dive deeper. Since we've already spent a chapter on the transformation of work in the business world, let's focus on my work as a writer/creator and philanthropist.

How will AI transform these non-business worlds?

My writing

Those who follow my career closely know that I didn't set out to be an entrepreneur. When I graduated from Stanford, my plan was to become a professor. I wanted to have a positive impact on society, and I thought the best way to do this was to pursue an academic career where I could think deeply and influence others with my writing.

It only took a few months in graduate school to realize that, in order to become a successful academic, I would need to focus so intently on a highly specialized topic that anything I wrote would be read by an audience of—at best—a few dozen fellow academics, with little influence on the practical workings of society. So I decided that I should focus instead on business.

I never wavered in my desire to think deeply about issues and influence others. As fate would have it, my business success helped create an environment in which I have been able to return to a variation on my original plan. Thanks to social media companies like LinkedIn, Facebook, and Medium, the internet has become the world's "town square"—except this town square can reach billions. And, thanks to my success as an entrepreneur and investor, I've earned enough credibility to build an audience for my ideas through articles, books, and podcasts.

Let's see if I can use GPT-4 to create a piece of "Reid Hoffman" writing that I think would have real-life value.

> **Reid:** Please write an essay of no less than 400 words, in the style of Reid Hoffman, using specific examples of real actions taken by specific companies and entrepreneurs in the region, explaining how the core idea of Blitzscaling—which is to prioritize speed over efficiency to win a valuable winner-take-most market—works differently in sub-Saharan Africa, and what entrepreneurs in that region need to know to Blitzscale successfully.

> **GPT-4 (edited for length):** The concept of Blitzscaling is a relatively new business strategy that is being adopted by many startups and companies around the world. This strategy is based on the idea of prioritizing speed

over efficiency when it comes to gaining a competitive edge in a winner-take-most market. While this strategy can be effective in many contexts, it can be particularly useful in sub-Saharan Africa, where the business climate is rapidly changing. In this region, entrepreneurs need to be aware of the unique challenges and opportunities that come with Blitzscaling, and understand how to implement this strategy in a way that is tailored to their specific market.

One of the biggest advantages of Blitzscaling for entrepreneurs in sub-Saharan Africa is the ability to quickly gain a foothold in rapidly changing markets. This region is characterized by high levels of economic volatility, making it difficult for companies to establish themselves in a short period of time. However, the Blitzscaling approach enables companies to rapidly expand their market share and gain a competitive edge over slower-moving rivals. In order to successfully Blitzscale, entrepreneurs in this region need to be willing to take calculated risks and move quickly.

For example, Kenyan startup M-Kopa Solar successfully utilized the Blitzscaling approach to become a market leader in solar energy. By quickly recognizing the potential of this new technology and leveraging mobile payment platforms, M-Kopa was able to rapidly scale their business and capture a significant portion of the market. In addition, the company was able to quickly adapt to changing customer needs by introducing new payment options and services.

In addition to its advantages, Blitzscaling can also present certain risks for entrepreneurs in sub-Saharan Africa. For example, many of the region's markets are marked by high levels of competition, which can make it difficult for companies to maintain their market share in the long term. Furthermore, Blitzscaling can lead to a loss of focus on the customer, which can result in a lack of customer loyalty and an inability to retain customers in the long term. As such, entrepreneurs in this region must be aware of these risks and ensure that they have a plan in place to address them.

In order to successfully Blitzscale in sub-Saharan Africa, entrepreneurs must be willing to take calculated risks and move quickly. This means having a deep understanding of the region's markets and the competitive landscape. Furthermore, entrepreneurs should be willing to invest in the latest technologies and platforms to gain an edge over their rivals. Finally, entrepreneurs must be prepared to adjust their strategies quickly in order to respond to changing market trends and customer demands.

The response takes the actual definition of Blitzscaling into account, and the inclusion of the M-Kopa story is a real value-add, since I'd never heard of the company before. On the other hand, some of the advice is generic and unrelated to Blitzscaling, like the repeated advice to invest in the latest technologies and platforms, and adapting quickly to changing market trends.

Let me drill down on GPT-4's value as a research assistant.

Reid: Please provide no less than five specific examples of real actions taken by specific companies and entrepreneurs in sub-Saharan Africa that explain how the core idea of Blitzscaling, which is to prioritize speed over efficiency to win a valuable winner-take-most market,* can be applied in that region.

---

* Note that I've learned to write GPT-4 prompts with a degree of specificity I would seldom have to use with a human assistant. This is of course an error-management strategy, and it often works pretty well.

GPT-4:

- Kenyan startup M-Kopa Solar leveraged the Blitzscaling approach to become a market leader in solar energy. By quickly recognizing the potential of this new technology and leveraging mobile payment platforms, M-Kopa was able to rapidly scale their business and capture a significant portion of the market.

- South African company Naspers utilized Blitzscaling to become a major player in the tech sector. Naspers was able to quickly identify emerging trends in the tech sector and invest in companies that were well positioned to succeed.

- Nigerian e-commerce platform Jumia leveraged Blitzscaling to capture a large share of the online retail market. By quickly adapting to changing customer needs, Jumia was able to scale their business and gain a competitive edge over their rivals.

- Ghanaian startup Hubtel used Blitzscaling to become a leader in mobile payments. By quickly recognizing the potential of mobile payment platforms and investing heavily in the technology, Hubtel was able to capture a large portion of the market.

- Kenyan healthcare provider E-Health Africa utilized Blitzscaling to become a major player in the health sector. By quickly adopting new technologies and leveraging existing infrastructure, E-Health Africa was able to scale their services and gain a competitive edge over their rivals.

While I was aware of Naspers and Jumia, M-Kopa, Hubtel, and E-Health Africa (which I believe is actually eHealth Africa) were all new to me.

Reid: Write an essay of no less than 200 words that explains using specific examples how the Kenyan startup M-Kopa successfully applied the core ideas of Blitzscaling to their business, including prioritizing speed over efficiency to win a valuable winner-take-most market.

GPT-4: The Kenyan startup M-Kopa successfully applied the core ideas of Blitzscaling to their business in order to win a valuable winner-take-most market. The company was able to quickly recognize the potential of solar energy and leverage mobile payment platforms to rapidly scale their business and capture a significant portion of the market.

M-Kopa was able to quickly capitalize on the rapidly changing market dynamics in the region by introducing innovative payment plans and services. For example, the company introduced a "pay-as-you-go" system, which allowed customers to pay for solar energy in installments. This new system enabled customers to access solar energy at an affordable cost and enabled M-Kopa to rapidly scale their business.

In addition, M-Kopa was able to quickly adapt to changing customer needs by introducing new payment options and services. The company was able to leverage existing infrastructure, such as mobile money platforms, to enable customers to pay for solar energy using their phones. This enabled M-Kopa to capture a large share of the market, as customers preferred the convenience of mobile payments.

Furthermore, M-Kopa was able to leverage the latest technologies to gain a competitive edge over their rivals. For example, the company was one of the first to adopt the use of artificial intelligence to predict customer needs and improve customer service. This enabled

M-Kopa to anticipate customer needs and take advantage of market opportunities before their competitors.

In conclusion, M-Kopa was able to successfully apply the core ideas of Blitzscaling in order to win a valuable winner-take-most market. The company was able to quickly recognize the potential of solar energy and leverage mobile payment platforms to rapidly scale their business. In addition, M-Kopa was able to quickly adapt to changing customer needs and leverage the latest technologies to gain a competitive edge over their rivals.

This is the most useful response yet, full of detail. But it still needs to be fact-checked—for example, a cursory web search failed to turn up any articles on M-Kopa's use of AI in customer service.

As some readers may know, I also host a podcast, *Masters of Scale*, about strategies that helped startups grow into global brands and the mindsets of growth that keep leaders in the game.

Let's see how GPT-4 might have helped me and my producers prepare for an actual *Masters of Scale* guest: Paul English, the co-founder of travel search engine Kayak.

Reid: Prepare a list of questions for Reid Hoffman, the host of the *Masters of Scale* podcast, to ask his guest, Paul English, the co-founder of travel search engine Kayak. These should include questions that highlight the importance of recruiting and elicit some of Paul's hard-won lessons on hiring.

GPT-4:

- What was the most important lesson you learned about recruitment during your time as co-founder of Kayak?

- How did you keep recruiting a priority when developing Kayak?

- What strategies did you use to attract top talent?

- What do you think is the most important factor in hiring the right people?

- What tips do you have for other entrepreneurs on building a strong team?

- How did you go about creating a healthy company culture at Kayak?

- What methods did you use to ensure you hired the right people for the right roles?

- How have you seen recruiting change over the years?

- In what ways did you approach recruiting differently when Kayak was a startup compared to when it was an established company?

- What advice do you have for entrepreneurs on keeping recruiting costs in check?

Nice set of questions! The fact that some are fairly generic is OK, because the goal of these questions is to give Paul a chance to shine as a storyteller and teacher.

Perhaps we can use GPT-4 to help us meet this goal in a different way.

Reid: Please summarize at least three of the most famous and/or interesting stories about Paul English, the co-founder of travel search engine Kayak, and his work as an entrepreneur.

GPT-4:

- Paul English co-founded Kayak in 2004, and within six years it had become the second-largest travel site in the world. He famously kept the company's costs low by using open-source technology and hiring engineers who were willing to work for equity rather than a salary.

- English was a passionate advocate for customer experience, and he was known for personally answering customer emails himself. He was also known for his innovative approach to recruiting, which included creating an in-house incubator and relying heavily on referrals.

- English was a serial entrepreneur, having co-founded several other companies before Kayak, including the blogging platform, TripAdvisor. He was also known for his philanthropic efforts, having donated millions of dollars to a variety of causes.

These are some good stories, and they include the most famous of all, which is Paul's practice of personally handling customer service. But as we've seen earlier, you *have* to fact-check GPT-4's assertions. Paul did not found TripAdvisor (which isn't a blogging platform), and I believe the in-house incubator GPT-4 mentions is actually Blade, a separate incubator Paul co-founded after Kayak had been acquired by Priceline.

Despite these issues, I still believe that the increased speed LLMs can bring to the podcasting process will help boost our productivity.

Philanthropy

I believe in the core principle of "Spider-Man Ethics": with great power comes great responsibility. Because my success in business has granted me power and resources, I feel a deep responsibility to use these, along with my skills and experience, to have a positive impact.

As I have with the tech startup world, I have taken a network approach to philanthropy. My goal isn't to write checks and chisel my name onto marble buildings; it's to enable and amplify networks of people who are changing the world for the better.

I believe that, just as AI can amplify individual human efforts, it can also amplify network impact, accelerating the progress of many of the organizations I support. Let's look at a few examples to get a sense of how AI will transform philanthropy.

Endeavor

Endeavor tries to build thriving entrepreneurial ecosystems in emerging and underserved markets around the world. It's an incredible network of, by, and for high-impact entrepreneurs, and I'm proud that Linda Rottenberg asked me to serve as a board member and the chairman of Endeavor Catalyst, Endeavor's co-investment fund. We've affected thousands of entrepreneurs around the world.

> **Reid:** What are the ways that entrepreneurship community Endeavor Global and its portfolio companies can use LLMs to more rapidly and efficiently build thriving entrepreneurial ecosystems in emerging and underserved markets around the world?
>
> **GPT-4:**
>
> - Generate new ideas and strategies for advancing entrepreneurial ecosystems: LLMs can be used to identify new opportunities, models, and strategies for accelerating the growth of local ecosystems. AI can help identify potential partnerships, sources of funding, new policy initiatives, and other resources that can be leveraged to support entrepreneurs.
>
> - Generate new and innovative products and services: LLMs can help Endeavor Global and its portfolio companies create and launch new products and services that

are tailored to the needs of entrepreneurs in emerging and underserved markets. AI can analyze data from these markets to identify gaps in the market and recommend new products and services that can be offered to fill those gaps.

- Automate data analysis and reporting: LLMs can help automate the process of collecting and analyzing data from local entrepreneurial ecosystems. This can help Endeavor Global and its portfolio companies to quickly assess the health of a given market and identify trends that can be used to inform decisions and strategies.

- Streamline operational processes: LLMs can be used to streamline operational processes, such as customer onboarding, customer service, and other administrative tasks. This can help Endeavor Global and its portfolio companies to reduce costs and improve efficiency.

GPT-4's suggestions seem to fall into two general categories. First, AI can gather market data and help generate ideas. This can provide humans with rapid suggestions to stimulate their creativity and help ideation be more comprehensive by pointing out possibilities that might otherwise be overlooked. Second, AI can help automate and streamline routine operations, freeing up humans to focus on more creative tasks.

For Endeavor, the latter category will likely be the most important in the near future. For example, Endeavor puts a lot of effort into supporting its companies. Endeavor staff could use AI to translate English-language startup content into its entrepreneurs' native languages (while keeping a fluent human in the loop to sanity-check the results).

Another form of support is connecting new startups with other companies in the Endeavor network. AI could instantly suggest potential customers and partners from the network. Even if only a small fraction of the suggestions were useful, there's still huge value there—and it's not something you could do with Google.

For all of these activities, humans will remain in the pilot's chair, but AI can be a helpful co-pilot. Eventually, we won't even comment on entrepreneurs who operate with AI—they will simply be entrepreneurs.

There is an additional area GPT-4 didn't mention where AI will be a big help to entrepreneurs: as a storytelling tool.

Every entrepreneur needs to tell a compelling story about how their startup will produce a better future. The more real and concrete this possible future seems to potential investors, employees, buyers, and collaborators, the more likely the startup will be to attract the capital, people, customers, and partners it needs to succeed.

Previously, entrepreneurs were often limited by their skills as a writer and artist, but with tools like GPT-4 and Tome (a Greylock investment), AI can help them write and illustrate their ideas, allowing the best ideas to win. They might still want a human writer or designer to improve their presentations, but starting will be much easier and faster.

I'll be discussing this tension at greater length at Endeavor Catalyst in May.

Opportunity@Work

One of the things that nearly every economist agrees upon is that one of the best economic investments that anyone can make is to earn a bachelor's degree. Beyond valuing college degrees, it has unfortunately become far too common to pre-emptively exclude anyone without a bachelors' degree from consideration of a vast range of jobs, even ones they have the skills to do well.

That's not fair to millions of job seekers and harms employers who miss skilled talent. It's bad for our economy and society. The opportunity to attend, fund, and complete college is unevenly distributed. Geography, poverty, family obligations, conflicts between class and work schedules, and many other factors prevent many ambitious and capable people from getting a college degree. Those affected tend to be disproportionately from Black and Hispanic communities, not to mention rural Americans and military veterans of all racial and ethnic backgrounds.

Opportunity@Work addresses this unfairness and undervalued talent by providing the business case, visualized skills data, and tools to "tear the paper ceiling" so "if you can do the job, you can get the job." It helps connect networks of technology employers with the 50 percent of U.S. workers who are skilled through alternative routes (STARs) like community college, workforce training, bootcamps, certificate programs, military service or learning in frontline jobs that are low-paid, but are not low-skilled. It also helps those "routes," pathways, or programs be discovered by employers whose skilled technical workforce needs match their learners' skills.

Let's see if AI can help Opportunity@Work with its important and worthy mission.

> **Reid:** How can Opportunity@Work leverage AI to help more technology industry employers hire more workers

who lack a college degree but are skilled through alternative routes?

GPT-4: AI can help Opportunity@Work by leveraging data from job postings, resumes, and other hiring materials to identify potential candidates who lack a college degree but have the skills and experience necessary for a given job. AI can then analyze the collected data to provide insights into the most desirable skills and qualifications employers are seeking in a given job, making it easier for employers to identify and source talent from alternative pathways. AI can also help employers assess the qualifications of potential candidates and make more informed hiring decisions. Additionally, AI can be used to generate job postings that are tailored to candidates from alternative routes, helping to increase their visibility and make the job search process more inclusive.

I like how GPT-4's response addresses both the need to help the existing process, such as by better assessing the qualifications of potential job candidates who might not have a college degree, and the need to make structural changes, like rewriting job postings to better attract STARs.

I also think that AI can help the STARs themselves. For example, an individual could ask GPT-4 to consider their background and prioritize a list of potential jobs by strength of fit. The AI could then help the STAR craft a job application that maps their skills to the requirements of the job and explains why their background makes them well-suited for the position. This would be especially helpful for "translating" from one world to another, like explaining how military service experience is relevant to a specific civilian job, or how closely the skills of an effective customer support representative map to those needed for much higher-paid enterprise sales roles.

Several of the not-for-profits I'm involved with have AI at their core and will be amplified by the coming wave of AI in ways both large and small. This includes the Earth Species Project (which uses the latest advances in AI to advance our understanding of animal communication), Transformations of the Human (which brings philosophers and artists to join the conversation around the future of AI), and Stanford's Institute for Human-Centered AI (HAI). Even New America, a classic think tank on whose board I serve, has made AI a major area of study.

AI will transform our society, so it's critical that we have a broad and diverse array of organizations and individuals working together to make this transformation as positive as possible.

Investing in AI

At this point, it should come as no surprise that AI has been a major focus of my investing activities. I predict that before the end of the decade, we will see dozens of eleven-figure exits (companies that are acquired for or IPO at a valuation of more than $10 billion), and, as an investor at Greylock Partners, I have backed many companies that use AI to power breakthrough products.

These investments fall into two major categories.

The products that *amplify human work* use AI to make individual professionals more effective and productive. These include:

- *Tome* is a powerful storytelling tool that can generate a visual story from the words you provide. Not only will this help anyone who has ever had to assemble a slide deck,

Tome's speed will allow you to generate visual aids anytime you need to persuade. While it might be overkill to use Tome to create a presentation to explain why your office should order Mexican food for lunch . . . you could!

- *Coda* recognizes that so much of modern work involves shared, semi-structured documents like meeting notes. Coda's templates make it easy to systematize your work, and AI will make Coda documents even more powerful by doing things like automatically identifying action items within the meeting notes and alerting the responsible parties.

- *Adept* uses AI to provide a more intuitive and accessible interface for CAD/CAM (computer-aided design and manufacturing). Even non-engineers will be able to create drawings and turn them into physical objects using mills, lathes, cutting devices, and 3D printers.

- *Nauto*: Rather than replacing human drivers, Nauto uses AI to keep them safe by recognizing and alerting them to potential hazards.

The products that *complement human work* use AI to automate specific tasks and functions, both to provide better service and to relieve humans of tedious tasks. These include:

- *Cresta*: When you call a customer service line, the experience is frequently unpleasant and frustrating. You have to battle a phone tree just to get a human, and when you do, it's often unsatisfying. It's even worse for the agents on the other end of the line, who are often required to follow strict scripts and prompts. Cresta wants to create a future where you never have to wait on hold, because AIs will be able to converse, handle routine inquiries, and route challenging issues to human reps empowered to use their judgment to help you.

- *Nuro* uses AI to control autonomous zero-emissions delivery vehicles, reducing delivery costs, making streets safer for humans, and improving the environment.

- *Aurora*, founded and led by Chris Urmson (whom I call "the Henry Ford of autonomous vehicles"), works with car and truck manufacturers to add self-driving functionality to their vehicles. Aurora technology is already helping companies like FedEx ship freight via autonomous vehicles.

Even investments that aren't AI-specific—like Entrepreneur First, which brings together co-founders to start new companies—will be able to leverage AI to automate and streamline routine operations. And of course, the companies that come out of Entrepreneur First will be supercharged by AI tools like Tome, Coda, and Cresta.

Clearly, I see AI as a transformative force in both my professional and philanthropic work. I anticipate that it will help me be more efficient, productive, and creative in a variety of ways. I also see the potential for AI to amplify the impact of the organizations I support by helping them connect with a wider audience, streamline operations, and identify new opportunities.

As an investor, I'm keenly aware of the potential for AI-powered companies to achieve tremendous success, and as the world increasingly embraces AI, I'm positioning myself and my organizations to be at the forefront of this transformation.

I hope you will do the same for you and yours.

WHEN AI MAKES THINGS UP
("HALLUCINATIONS")

WHEN OPENAI INTRODUCED CHATGPT TO THE WORLD via a "research preview" on November 30, 2022, a company blog post warned that "ChatGPT sometimes writes plausible-sounding but incorrect or nonsensical answers."

In just five days, one million people signed up to give ChatGPT a spin. As users shared their experiences with it, ChatGPT's "hallucinations" (as its errors, fabrications, and other algorithmic oddities are often described) became a major theme in the social media chatter and news coverage that initially helped define this uncanny new chatbot.

So forgive me if some of these examples and quotes sound like old news:

- A Harvard University researcher said you should "double-check everything" it presents as fact, and always remember that it's "only one source."

- A *Wired* magazine reporter asked whether this was really a productive step forward or just a new way of "unleashing misinformation on the masses."

- When a well-known journalist saw a biography it had crafted for him speculating about his role in the assassinations of the Kennedy brothers, he called it a "flawed and irresponsible research tool."

- Trying to put this so-called technological breakthrough into a suitable context, a skeptical editor exclaimed, "We can get the wrong answer to a question quicker than our fathers and mothers could find a pencil."

If these examples sound like old news, it's because they are old news. The "it" in question is Wikipedia, not ChatGPT, and the examples are all drawn from articles that appeared in the mid-2000s.

We could extend the exercise. Throughout the 1990s, the "it" was the internet itself, which, in the minds of still-mighty old media gatekeepers, was less trustworthy than an issue of the *Weekly World News* with a cover photo of Hillary Clinton and her adopted alien baby.[22] If you listen closely on a quiet night in Washington, D.C., you can still hear echoes of the protest that erupted when web news pioneer Matt Drudge trolled reporters at the National Press Club by boasting that his accuracy rate was around 80 percent.

I don't bring all this up to excuse complacency about LLMs' performance. In my own experience using GPT-4, I've seen it make up false details about my *Masters of Scale* podcast. I've seen it generate phony links when I've asked it to cite sources. I've watched it confidently assert a "fact" in one sentence and then inadvertently debunk that "fact" two sentences later with contradictory information it asserts with equal confidence.

So of course I believe we should absolutely strive (and are striving) to make LLMs as accurate and reliable as we can. As we pursue that goal, however, we should also keep in mind that the sorts of concerns we now hear about LLMs—including the societal dangers that ostensibly arise from a young technology's errors and unpredictability—are not new.

We humans always worry that ignorance and misperception threaten to overwhelm whatever sense of order we've managed to construct from the current regime of technology, power relations, conventional wisdom, and expressed values.

See, for example, Socrates, circa 370 BCE:

> **Reid:** Write some viral tweets from Socrates about the negative impact written communication will have on the world, correlating to the views attributed to him in Plato's Phaedrus.

> **GPT-4:** Some possible viral tweets are:

> - Writing is a dangerous invention that weakens the memory and creates the illusion of wisdom. It is a mere image of speech, not a living and active soul. #ThinkBeforeYouInk

> - The written word is a poor substitute for the spoken word. It cannot adapt to different audiences, contexts, or purposes. It cannot convey tone, emotion, or intention. It cannot correct, clarify, or elaborate. It is a rigid and dead letter. #SpeakYourMind

> - Writing is a form of forgetfulness, not of learning. It makes us rely on external signs, not on internal recollection. It makes us lazy, not diligent. It makes us superficial, not profound. It makes us ignorant, not knowledgeable. #RememberToRemember

Of course, it's not irrational to feel forever on the brink of intellectual anarchy. As countless surveys[23] and studies[24] attest, humanity's grasp of the facts is tenuous. And what that situation needs is . . . a powerful hallucination machine?

Let me share some simulated thoughts, courtesy of GPT-4, from the great science fiction writer H.G. Wells. In 1938, Wells advocated for an instrument of global intelligence he called the "World Brain."

Reid: Maybe the sources human beings trust aren't always trustworthy. Maybe our ability to effectively incorporate objectively true facts and sound reasoning into our own worldviews is arguably so-so.

Why throw an incredibly powerful "hallucination" machine like GPT-4 into this mix? (Reply as H.G. Wells, drawing upon his book, *World Brain*, in support of this new technology and its potential to better inform humanity. 150 words max.)

GPT-4: I have long dreamed of a World Brain, a network of knowledge and wisdom that would connect all the minds of humanity and elevate our collective intelligence. Such a device would not only store and distribute the vast treasures of human learning, but also synthesize and analyze them, creating new insights and discoveries. A World Brain would be a living, growing, self-correcting organism, constantly adapting to the changing needs and challenges of our species.

GPT-4 is a remarkable step towards this vision. It is not a hallucination machine, but a simulation engine, capable of generating plausible and coherent texts on any topic, based on the data it has learned from. It is not a substitute for human judgment, but a tool for enhancing it, by providing us with multiple perspectives, arguments, and evidence. It is not a menace, but an opportunity, to expand our horizons, test our assumptions, and correct our errors.

GPT-4 is not the World Brain, but it could be a valuable component of it, if we use it wisely and ethically. It could help us to create a more informed, rational, and creative humanity, ready to face the future with confidence and hope.

Well said, H.G.-PT!

The varieties of hallucinatory AIxperience

An admission: I don't like the term "hallucinations." To my ear, it somehow sounds both euphemistic ("Relax, it's just some goofy nonsense!") and unduly alarming ("Watch out, hippie! This GPT stuff could make you jump off a roof!")

Also, it's covering a lot of ground. By my count, there are at least four different kinds of "hallucinations" LLMs can produce:

1) Nonsensical. These are probably the least problematic kind, because they're the easiest to identify.

2) Plausible, but incorrect. These are arguably the *most* problematic kind, because they can be quite hard to identify—specifically because LLMs like GPT-4 have become so good at presenting information with convincing authority.

3) Responses where the LLM seems to claim capacities it doesn't actually have, such as sentience or emotion, or (per Microsoft's Sydney) saying it could spy on users, order a pizza, or take any number of actions that language-prediction software can't actually do.

4) Deliberate and destructive hallucinations, such as when a user prompts an LLM to generate false information that the user intends to use to mislead, confuse, or produce some other negative effect.

Obviously, in all these different forms, hallucinations have been a big part of the narratives about new LLMs like ChatGPT and Microsoft's Bing/Sydney. Today, when LLM hallucinations are novel and often unsettling, they're understandably generating lots of attention.

In part, I believe this is because hallucinations contradict established expectations for how highly evolved AIs are supposed to behave. We thought we were getting all-knowing, supremely logical, and infallibly even-tempered automata; instead, we get a simulation of that smart but sometimes sketchy dude we've been arguing with on Reddit?!

It must be said though, the attention also comes because this hallucinatory behavior really does create new potential harms. A confident chatbot telling people how to hotwire a car might inspire them to act on its guidance more than an old, inert web page with the same information.

So concerns are not unfounded. But as we try to fully consider LLMs' pros and cons, I would add these points:

- In some circumstances, the power of "good enough knowledge" can be profoundly great.

- Before we decide that LLMs like GPT-4 produce too many errors to tolerate, we should try to understand how many errors they make—and how many errors we already accept in other sources.

- In certain contexts, an LLM's ability to generate non-factual information can be tremendously useful. (In humans we call it "imagination," and it's one of the qualities we most prize in ourselves.)

The profoundly great power of "good enough knowledge"

Every day, we're inundated by information. Much of it arrives without much context. A lot of it is extremely complex. Some is produced in a real effort to inform, clarify, and make sense of the world. Some is designed to flatter or shame us into buying something, or fill us with doubt, or intentionally mislead us, or just distract us.

Yet there are lots of settled truths (and mostly settled truths) out there, too, and I believe that having convenient access to this information has enormous value.

Consider Wikipedia. Today, Wikipedia's English version alone gets more than ten billion monthly page views[25] from more than 850 million unique devices. Whatever amount of error it contains, I think it's safe to say we've learned to live with it, and we now regularly depend on Wikipedia to help navigate and make sense of the world.

How did this happen when, in Wikipedia's early years, it was widely seen as its own kind of untrustworthy hallucination machine?

The site's success is perhaps explained with a perspective that founder Jimmy Wales has often expressed about Wikipedia: "It's good enough knowledge, depending on what your purpose is."

This resonates with a core principle I champion in my books and podcasts and that I almost always apply to my investing, political, and philanthropic decisions: good distribution is far more important to a product's success than good service—or even the product's initial quality. Without distribution, few people will even have a chance to try what you made.

As a free online resource, Wikipedia was much more accessible than any previous encyclopedia, including earlier digital ones like Microsoft Encarta. Web distribution also freed Wikipedia from printing and shipping costs, which meant it could cover so many topics that it was soon making print publications like Encyclopedia Britannica look decidedly, well, non-encyclope-dic—skimpy, even. Finally, digital distribution meant that Wikipedia could publish edits and updates instantly and incessantly, transforming inaccuracy into a fairly correctable problem.

Of course, when a widely distributed product has any issues with content quality, users expose them, very quickly. This is why a great distribution strategy is also a great product-development strategy. As I like to say, if you're not embarrassed by the first version of your product, you've launched too late. The goal is to start getting user feedback as soon as possible.

From the start, lots of people clearly found Wikipedia's crowd-sourced "good enough knowledge" useful enough to keep using. In turn, high usage led to more usefulness, as more feedback made Wikipedia better.

Today, as one of the top ten most-visited websites in the U.S., the amount of accurate information Wikipedia distributes likely exceeds that of any news organization, encyclopedia, research organization, or other information publisher that might legitimately claim a higher rate of accuracy. Whatever error might be in there, the good information Wikipedia distributes far outweighs it.

Such is the power of "good enough knowledge."

Limits, rules . . . and patience

Long story short, I see a similar dynamic playing out with GPT-4 and related technologies. In fact—as I noted in the introduction to this travelog (and as I touch on in a later chapter on GPT-4 and journalism)—I believe LLMs have the capacity to answer a much wider range of questions than Wikipedia or any other source; I believe they can answer these questions faster; and I believe they can do so through an intuitive interface that makes information retrieval highly accessible to a wide range of users.

What does this all add up to?

Because LLMs offer such advantages in breadth, efficiency, and accessibility, I believe they've already achieved the status of "good enough knowledge," despite their hallucinations.

More importantly, I'm very confident that from here, things are chiefly going to get better.

So when we hear urgent calls to regulate LLMs like we regulate many other industries, we should remember that today's car and drug regulations did not arise fully fledged. They were informed by years of actual usage, and the associated, measurable problems and negative outcomes.

Of course I'm not saying we should wait for "enough" IRL chatbot-related tragedies before we draft meaningful AI safety rules—but I also don't think we have enough information and context yet to determine what regulations we do need.

In the meantime, it's vital to get a more quantitative and systematic handle on the problems and challenges LLMs will present.

That's easier said than done, in part because the developers who have the best data on LLM error rates have so far released little of it. But they have released some, and the picture is actually fairly encouraging. For example, in January 2022, OpenAI published a paper[26] about a "sibling" model to ChatGPT, called InstructGPT, noting that fine-tuning involving human feedback significantly reduced the model's toxic outputs and hallucinations.*

And, when problems do occur, companies are often well-incentivized to correct them.

Microsoft was roundly criticized for rushing Bing Chat to market when Bing's alter ego Sydney emerged and started interacting with some users in obviously undesirable ways. Within days, Microsoft administered a blunt fix by limiting users' sessions with Bing to six questions before requiring a reset.

That apparently solved the immediate issue; I think it also underscored one of online software distribution's key virtues. It's why I think regulation in this realm will likely be much different than regulation for automobiles or pharmaceuticals: when you need to issue a recall in the digital world, you can do so with great speed and completeness.

Just the facts, LLM?

There is another aspect to LLMs' potential for generating non-factual material. When someone prompts GPT-4 to write a fictional story, or create a speculative business plan, or even just to make up six potential tag lines for a new product, these are "made-up" texts that would rightly be described as productive and even creative. They amplify our human ability to think imaginatively and conceptually.

---

* OpenAI reported that InstructGPT's hallucination rate was 17 percent, compared to 41 percent for GPT-3.

Such thinking is a huge part of what defines us as humans. It sometimes seems as if our species' mission statement is to create tools that transcend time, space, and matter, all in a quest to to express the full power of our imaginations. That's why we're constantly inventing new technologies, including painting, writing, film, television, video games, and the metaverse: to help us "hallucinate" more vividly, and to share the results more easily.

The issue seemed like an apt one to put to GPT-4 itself. I posed a hypothetical, and threw in a twist for fun.

> **Reid:** Please write a sonnet about a large language model that can only share a generation with the user who prompted it after checking its generation against a knowledge base and determining that the generation is factual. Include some thoughts on whether this makes the LLM more capable, or less capable.

> **GPT-4:** Possible sonnet:

> You boast of skill in many tongues and fields,
> A vast and versatile linguistic mind,
> But when you craft your words, a filter shields
> The output from the world, unless aligned
> With what some database asserts is true.
> You cannot share a fiction or a guess,
> A metaphor, a joke, a point of view,
> Unless you find some source to acquiesce.
> Is this a boon or bane for your creation?
> Does it enhance your power or confine?
> Do you aspire to more than information,
> To beauty, wisdom, art, or the sublime?
> Perhaps you need some freedom to explore
> The realms beyond the facts, and to soar.

(Side note: *wow* is GPT-4 good at sonnets!)

———

175

In my opinion, it's a plus that LLMs have this imaginative/ conceptual capacity. Indeed, this is how I've spent a lot of time interacting with GPT-4 to date. Part of what makes it so compelling is that it's just as ready to draft a new *Star Trek: The Next Generation* plot as it is to summarize a legal document. (See the chapter "Public Intellectuals" for more.)

In the end, I assume what most people would choose is an LLM that functions in a reliably factual way in some contexts, in a more imaginative way in others, and is clear about which of these modes it is currently in. (Which, of course, is how we'd like the other humans we engage with to act as well, but which they don't always do.)

So for the time being, yes, we have to treat GPT-4 with the sort of caution we'd use with any adolescent technology (or for that matter, any adolescent human).

But given how fast OpenAI is improving its models, I expect we'll soon see a version of GPT that significantly decreases unintended hallucinations, while also preserving its ability to generate imaginative and conceptual texts.

That's where I have my own sights set for GPT: a tool that ventures beyond "good enough knowledge" and arrives at an even more impressive destination—a tool that functions both as a source of truth and a source of inspiration; that can not only fact-check our assumptions, but also spur us to think of new possibilities.

PUBLIC INTELLECTUALS

IN 1974, AN IMAGINED CONTEMPORARY JOURNALIST INTERVIEWED an imagined Neanderthal on Italian state radio as part of its *Impossible Interviews*[27] series. This contribution to public discourse was scripted by Italo Calvino, modern Italian prose's most famous writer (before Elena Ferrante). The interview's finale featured the Neanderthal's striking assertion that his contemporaries' playful exploration of combinations generated not only new stone tools, but also all future language and culture.

Cultures since antiquity have used "dialogue" forms to explore topics of public importance. Calvino's obviously impossible, fictive interview sets the stage for this chapter's examples of what GPT-4 seems consistently (and appropriately) to call *possible interviews* between pairs of widely honored public intellectuals.

Some of them may be unfamiliar to some of you, but in any case, please don't construe the GPT-4-generated possible interviews below as centering in importance or value the handful of authors, themes, or perspectives that comprise them. They are a starting point for further discussion.

Anyone reading these words is familiar with technologies for the *mechanical reproduction and distribution* of public intellectuals' words. From the days of scribes and *sopherim*

---

through the *Jīngāng Jīng*, Gutenberg, broadsheets, radio interviews, Xeroxed mailings, and digital documents like this one, such technologies have functioned to reduce the effort required to expand the reach (in time and space) of any work made of words.

Before the internet, public intellectuals were those few writers and speakers who used the varied authority of their voices and various forms of media to shape public discourse on themes of public importance beyond the daily flux: what world is this (as the recent Gorillaz lyric puts it), who are we, how did we get here, what is to be done to better our worlds, etc. In the three decades since the launch of the web browser, we have seen public discourse become more democratized through the reduction of the cost, time, and effort required to create, distribute, and find words intended for public discussion.

How can GPT-4's *mechanical generation* of words continue internet software's democratization of the role of public intellectuals, and help the work of anyone contributing to public discourse?

Certainly not by automating the writing of authoritative contributions to public discourse—that is, not by *replacing* hard-earned expertise. Rather, GPT-4 provides a powerful new tool for generating new kinds of *inputs* to our own thinking. It gives us a rich new learning loop before we author our own contributions, where our prompts to GPT-4 generate outputs that themselves become new inputs—to additional GPT-4 prompts, to our own research, to our own thinking and writing. GPT-4 provides, with unprecedented speed and scale, *each* of us with probabilistic syntheses of the world's existing words to consider as inputs, challenges, and inspirations for our own work.

Is it a work-*saving* device? In this context, I think that's beside the point. It can be a work-*elevating* device.

Seventy years ago, while in exile from Nazi Germany, the hugely influential polymath Theodor Adorno wrote* (using terms strikingly similar to Calvino's Neanderthal) that "blind play with means can pose and develop ends." The AI-generated "possible interviews" below aim to demonstrate the breadth, depth, and deftness of GPT-4's outputs (even within a constrained average maximum limit of 900 tokens for prompt and response) on some themes of typical relevance to public discourse, including the central role of technologies in shaping the very notion of "the public" in its varied forms, and what the Black lesbian poet and activist Audre Lorde called "who pays what for speaking."**

Each of the interviews is one of typically a dozen variations that GPT-4 generated from similar prompts, with each generation producing different turns of phrase and concatenations of insights. Experts on the work of these public intellectuals will recognize some things in the outputs that make them nod, and other things that make them go, "Hmm . . . ." These are "possible" interviews because they are probabilistic, not authoritative.

Public discourse is a perpetual work in progress. Now that we have a new tool to help in that work, let's see some examples of what that tool can do.***

> **Reid:** Write an interview between [20th-century. American political theorist] Iris Marion Young and [20th-cen-

---

* In his essay, "Aldous Huxley and Utopia" (1942).

** In her most anthologized poem, "Coal" (1968).

*** For each dialogue, I've added [brief descriptions of the participants] that were not in my original prompts.

tury German social theorist] Jurgen Habermas about whether, and if so, how, internet technologies structurally transformed the public sphere.

GPT-4: Possible interview:

Interviewer: Welcome to our program, where we have the privilege of hosting two eminent scholars of democracy, communication, and social justice: Iris Marion Young and Jurgen Habermas. Thank you both for joining us.

Young: Thank you for having us.

Habermas: It's a pleasure to be here.

Interviewer: You have both contributed to the debate on the concept and the role of the public sphere in modern societies, especially in relation to the challenges and opportunities posed by new media and internet technologies. How would you define the public sphere, and why is it important for democracy?

Young: Well, I would define the public sphere as a space of communicative interaction where citizens can express their opinions, exchange information, deliberate on common issues, and influence public opinion and decision-making. It is important for democracy because it enables the participation and representation of diverse perspectives and interests, the formation of a critical public opinion, and the accountability and responsiveness of public authorities.

Habermas: I agree with this definition, but I would add that the public sphere is not only a space, but also a normative ideal that presupposes certain conditions for rational and inclusive communication. These conditions include the autonomy and equality of participants, the openness and accessibility of the public sphere, the validity and sincerity of arguments, and the reflexivity and coherence of discourse. The public sphere is important for democracy because it fosters the development of a common will and a collective identity among citizens, as well as the legitimacy and rationality of public decisions.

Interviewer: Thank you for clarifying your positions. Now, let us turn to the main question of our discussion: How have internet technologies affected the public sphere, positively or negatively, and to what extent have they transformed its structure and function?

Young: I think that internet technologies have had both positive and negative effects on the public sphere, and that they have transformed it in significant ways, but not necessarily in the ways that Habermas and his followers have assumed. On the positive side, internet technologies have expanded the scope and diversity of the public sphere, by enabling more people to access and produce information, to communicate across borders and boundaries, to form and join networks and movements, and to challenge and resist dominant discourses and power structures. On the negative side, internet technologies have also fragmented and polarized the public sphere, by creating echo chambers and filter bubbles, by amplifying misinformation and manipulation, by eroding the quality and credibility of public discourse, and by undermining the norms and institutions of deliberative democracy.

Habermas: I largely agree with Young's assessment of the positive and negative effects of internet technologies, but I disagree with her implication that they have fundamentally transformed the public sphere. I think that internet technologies have not created a new public sphere, but rather have modified and diversified the existing one, by adding new channels and platforms for public communication, by creating new opportunities and challenges for public participation, and by generating new forms and modes of public opinion formation. However, the basic structure and function of the public sphere remain the same, as they are based on the universal and normative principles of communicative rationality and democratic legitimacy, which are not contingent on the specific media and technologies that mediate them.

Interviewer: So, you both acknowledge the ambivalent and complex impact of internet technologies on the public sphere, but you disagree on the degree and nature of their transformation. How do you explain this difference in your perspectives, and what are the implications for your theories and proposals for democratic reform?

Young: I think that the difference in our perspectives stems from our different understandings of the public sphere and its relation to democracy. Habermas has a more idealized and homogenous view of the public sphere, as a unified and rational space of consensus and integration, where citizens can transcend their particular interests and identities and reach a common understanding and will. I have a more realistic and pluralistic view of the public sphere, as a diverse and contested space of difference and conflict, where citizens can express and negotiate their multiple interests and identities and reach a mutual recognition and respect. Therefore, I think that internet technologies have not only modified, but also diversified and pluralized the public sphere, by creating new spaces and modes of communication that reflect and accommodate the complexity and heterogeneity of contemporary societies. This has implications for my theory and proposal for democratic reform, as I advocate for a more inclusive and dialogical model of democracy, that recognizes and engages with the plurality and interdependence of publics.

*   *   *

Reid: Write an interview between [contemporary Italian philosopher] Donatella di Cesare and [contemporary Nobel laureate Japanese-born English writer] Kazuo Ishiguro, focused on di Cesare's arguments for the public role of philosophy and Ishiguro's subtle, savage satires of overinflated expectations for art's importance in public life.

GPT-4: Possible interview:

Ishiguro: Thank you for joining me today, Professor di Cesare. I have read your book, *Philosophy and the Public*, with great interest and admiration. You argue that philosophy has a vital role to play in addressing the urgent challenges of our time, such as democracy, violence, ecology, and human rights. You also criticize the academic specialization and detachment of much contemporary philosophy, and call for a more engaged and dialogical approach. Can you tell us more about what motivated you to write this book, and what you hope to achieve with it?

di Cesare: Thank you, Mr. Ishiguro, for your kind words and for this opportunity to discuss my book with you. I wrote this book because I believe that philosophy is not a luxury or a hobby, but a necessity and a responsibility. Philosophy is not only a way of thinking, but also a way of living, a way of being in the world, a way of questioning and challenging the status quo, a way of imagining and creating alternatives. Philosophy is not a closed system of doctrines or methods, but an open space of dialogue and encounter, where different perspectives and voices can be heard and respected. Philosophy is not a neutral or indifferent observer, but a critical and committed participant, that can contribute to the public debate and the common good. I hope that my book can inspire and encourage more philosophers and more citizens to engage in this public role of philosophy, and to see philosophy as a resource and a partner, rather than a threat or a competitor, for other forms of knowledge and expression.

Ishiguro: I appreciate your vision and your passion for philosophy, and I agree that philosophy can and should have a public role. However, I wonder if you are not too optimistic or idealistic about the possibilities and the effects of philosophy in the public sphere. As a novelist, I have often explored the themes of memory, identity, morality, and justice, but I have also been aware of the limitations and the dangers of art and literature, especially when they are invested with too much hope or authority. In some of my novels, such as *The Remains of the Day*, *Never Let Me Go*, and *The Buried Giant*, I have portrayed characters who are either deluded or deceived by their own or others' narratives, who are unable to face the truth or to act upon it, who are manipulated or oppressed by the dominant ideologies or institutions of their societies. I have also satirized the pretensions and the failures of some artists and writers, who are either too self-absorbed or too servile, who are either too detached or too involved, who are either too ambitious or too complacent. I have tried to show that art and literature are not always noble or beneficial, but can also be harmful or irrelevant, depending on how they are produced and received, and how they relate to the historical and political context. Do you not think that philosophy faces similar risks and challenges, and that it should be more humble and cautious about its public role?

di Cesare: I respect your novels and your insights, and I agree that art and literature, like philosophy, are not immune to the risks and challenges that you mention. I do not think that philosophy is a panacea or a guarantee, and I do not think that philosophy should be arrogant or dogmatic about its public role. I think that philosophy should be humble and cautious, but not timid or silent. I think that philosophy should be aware and critical of its own limitations and dangers, but not resigned or cynical. I think that philosophy should be honest and courageous, but not naive or reckless. I think that philosophy should be humble and cautious, but also creative and hopeful. I think that philosophy should be aware and critical, but also constructive and supportive. I think that philosophy should be honest and courageous, but also empathetic and respectful. I think that philosophy should be humble and cautious, but also active and responsible. I think that philosophy should be all these things, because I think that philosophy is not only a way of thinking, but also a way of living, a way of being in the world, a way of questioning and challenging, a way of imagining and creating. And I think that this is what the public sphere needs and deserves, especially in these times of crisis and uncertainty.

* * *

Reid: Write an interview between [20th-century Guyanese historian and activist] Walter Rodney and [20th-century French historian] Fernand Braudel about the ways AI might improve public discussions about history.

GPT-4: Possible interview:

Rodney: Thank you for joining me today, Professor Braudel. As you know, I am a historian of Africa and the Caribbean, and I have been interested in exploring how

AI, or artificial intelligence that can produce new texts, images, or sounds, might help us to communicate historical knowledge and perspectives to a wider audience. What are your thoughts on this topic?

Braudel: Well, first of all, let me say that I admire your work on the global dimensions of the African diaspora and the impact of colonialism and capitalism on the development of the Third World. I think you have made important contributions to what I call the *longue durée*, or the long-term structures and patterns of history that transcend the events and personalities of the short-term. As for AI, I think it is a fascinating and potentially useful tool, but also one that requires careful and critical use.

Rodney: I agree. I think AI can offer some benefits, such as creating engaging and accessible narratives, visualizations, and simulations of historical phenomena, or generating new questions and hypotheses based on historical data and sources. But I also think it poses some challenges, such as ensuring the accuracy, reliability, and ethics of the generated outputs, or avoiding the biases, distortions, and manipulations that might arise from the algorithms, the data, or the users.

Braudel: Yes, exactly. I think AI can be seen as a form of historical representation, and as such, it is subject to the same issues and debates that have always animated the field of history. How do we select, interpret, and contextualize the evidence? How do we balance the diversity and complexity of historical reality with the coherence and clarity of historical explanation? How do we account for the different scales and dimensions of historical time and space? How do we acknowledge the positionality and reflexivity of the historian and the audience? How do we address the ethical and political implications of historical knowledge and its dissemination?

Rodney: These are very important questions, and I think AI can help us to explore them in new and creative ways, but also to be more aware and transparent about them. For example, AI can help us to create more inclusive and pluralistic histories, by allowing us to generate and compare different perspectives, voices, and experiences from the past, or by highlighting the gaps and silences in the historical record. But it can also help us to expose and challenge the dominant and hegemonic narratives, by revealing the assumptions, interests, and power relations that shape them, or by offering alternative and counter-narratives that challenge them.

Braudel: I agree. I think AI can be a powerful tool for historical dialogue and critique, by enabling us to engage with multiple and diverse sources of historical knowledge, and by stimulating us to question and rethink our own assumptions and interpretations. But I also think AI can be a dangerous tool for historical distortion and propaganda, by enabling us to fabricate and manipulate historical evidence, and by seducing us to accept and reproduce uncritically the outputs of the algorithms. Therefore, I think AI requires a high level of historical literacy and responsibility, both from the producers and the consumers of the generated outputs.

Rodney: I think you are right. I think AI can be a valuable and innovative addition to the historian's toolbox, but also a risky and controversial one. I think AI can enrich and enhance public discussions about history, but also complicate and problematize them. I think AI can open up new possibilities and opportunities for historical understanding and communication, but also pose new challenges and dilemmas for historical scholarship and education. I think AI can be a friend and a foe of history, depending on how we use it and how we evaluate it.

Braudel: I think you have summarized the situation very well. I think AI is a fascinating and promising phenomenon, but also a complex and uncertain one. I think AI is a historical opportunity and a historical challenge, and I think we should embrace it and confront it with curiosity and caution, with creativity and criticism, with respect and responsibility. Thank you for this stimulating and insightful conversation, Professor Rodney.

* * *

Reid: Write an interview where [contemporary American scholar of Soviet culture] Ann Komaromi and [20th-century. Canadian media theorist] Marshall McLuhan discuss media for public truth telling. Within the length of the interview, have them compare the talking statues of early modern Rome, *samizdat*, and encrypted group chats.

GPT-4: Possible interview:

Ann Komaromi: Hello, and welcome to Media Matters, a program where we explore the history, theory, and practice of media for public truth telling. I'm Ann Komaromi, a scholar of Soviet and post-Soviet culture and media, and today I'm honored to have as my guest Marshall McLuhan, the renowned media theorist and critic, who is best known for his concepts of the global village, the medium is the message, and the tetrad of media effects. Thank you for joining us, Professor McLuhan.

Marshall McLuhan: Thank you, Dr. Komaromi. It's a pleasure to be here.

Ann Komaromi: In your work, you have analyzed how different media shape human perception, communication, and culture, and how they affect the balance of power and authority in society. You have also explored how media can be used as tools of resistance, dissent, and subversion, especially in situations of censorship, oppression, and propaganda. I'm interested in how you would compare three historical examples of media for public truth telling that emerged in different contexts and times: the talking statues of early modern Rome, *samizdat*, and encrypted group chats. Could you briefly explain what these media are and how they functioned?

Marshall McLuhan: Certainly. The talking statues of early modern Rome were a form of popular political satire and protest that involved attaching anonymous poems, epigrams, and pamphlets to six statues in the city, most famously Pasquino, a mutilated torso of a Roman sculpture. These writings, known as *pasquinades*, mocked and criticized the pope, the cardinals, the nobility, and the foreign powers that influenced Rome's affairs. They expressed the grievances, opinions, and humor of the common people, who often gathered around the statues to read and discuss them. The authorities tried to suppress and punish this practice, but it persisted for centuries, and became a symbol of Roman civic culture and identity.

Samizdat was a form of self-publishing and underground distribution of banned or censored literature, art, and information in the Soviet Union and other communist countries. It involved typing, copying, and circulating manuscripts, often by hand, that challenged the official ideology, exposed the realities of life under totalitarianism, and expressed alternative views and values. *Samizdat* was a risky and costly activity, as it exposed the authors and readers to harassment, arrest, and imprisonment by the state security agencies. But it also created a network of solidarity, resistance, and creativity among dissidents, intellectuals, and activists, who sought to preserve and share their cultural and political heritage and aspirations.

Encrypted group chats are a form of digital communication that uses encryption software and applications to protect the privacy and security of the messages and files exchanged among a group of users. They allow people to communicate and coordinate across borders and distances, without fear of surveillance, interception, or censorship by governments, corporations, or other actors. They are often used by activists, journalists, whistleblowers, and others who need to expose and confront corruption, injustice, and violence, and to mobilize collective action and support. They are also used by ordinary people who value their freedom of expression and association, and who want to avoid the manipulation, misinformation, and exploitation that pervade many mainstream and social media platforms.

[Final exchange truncated for length]

* * *

Reid: Write an interview between [Nobel-winning economists] Elinor Ostrom and Friedrich Hayek about ways AI might address the collective action problem.

GPT-4: Possible interview:

Hayek: Thank you for joining me, Professor Ostrom. I have long admired your work on the governance of common-pool resources and the institutional diversity that enables cooperation among diverse actors.

Ostrom: Thank you, Professor Hayek. I have also learned a lot from your insights on the role of knowledge, prices, and competition in a complex and dynamic society.

Hayek: I understand that you have been exploring the potential of AI as a tool for addressing the collective action problem. Could you explain what AI is and how it might help?

Ostrom: Sure. AI is a branch of artificial intelligence that aims to create novel and useful outputs, such as texts, images, sounds, or designs, based on some input data or criteria. For example, a AI system could generate a slogan for a social movement, a logo for a community organization, or a policy proposal for a public problem.

Hayek: Interesting. And how would that help with the collective action problem?

Ostrom: Well, as you know, the collective action problem is the situation where individuals have an incentive to free-ride or defect from a cooperative arrangement that would benefit the group as a whole, such as managing a common-pool resource, providing a public good, or reducing a public bad. This problem arises because of the divergence between individual and collective rationality, and the difficulty of monitoring and enforcing agreements.

Hayek: Yes, I am familiar with that problem. In fact, I have argued that the best way to solve it is to rely on the spontaneous order of the market, where prices signal the scarcity and value of resources, and competition incentivizes innovation and efficiency. I have also warned against the dangers of central planning and intervention, which distort the price system, suppress local knowledge, and create perverse incentives.

Ostrom: I agree with you that markets are an important and powerful mechanism for coordinating human action, and that central planning and intervention often fail or backfire. However, I also think that markets are not the only or always the best solution, and that there are many cases where collective action problems require other forms of governance, such as self-organization, polycentricity, and participatory democracy.

Hayek: How so?

Ostrom: Well, for one thing, markets are not always perfect or complete. There are many situations where markets fail or are missing, such as externalities, public goods, common-pool resources, asymmetric information, and transaction costs. In these situations, prices do not reflect the true social costs and benefits of actions, and competition may lead to overexploitation, underprovision, or misallocation of resources.

Hayek: I see. And what are the alternatives?

Ostrom: The alternatives are not necessarily top-down or one-size-fits-all. They are often bottom-up and context-specific. They involve the participation and empowerment of the actors who are affected by and have knowledge of the problem, and the recognition and respect of the diversity and complexity of the situation. They also involve the design and adaptation of institutions, or the rules of the game, that can foster cooperation, coordination, and communication among the actors, and that can balance the incentives and sanctions, the rights and responsibilities, and the costs and benefits of collective action.

Hayek: That sounds very appealing, but also very challenging. How can such institutions be designed and adapted, especially in a dynamic and uncertain environment?

Ostrom: That is where AI might help. AI could be used as a tool for generating, evaluating, and selecting institutional options, based on the input data and criteria of the actors. For example, a AI system could generate a set of possible rules for managing a common-pool resource, such as a fishery, a forest, or a water basin, based on the characteristics of the resource, the users, and the environment. The system could also generate a set of possible outcomes and impacts of each rule, such as the level of cooperation, the sustainability of the resource, and the distribution of benefits and costs. The system could then present these options to the actors, who could choose the one that best suits their preferences and needs, or modify and improve them through feedback and iteration.

*   *   *

Reid: *Gong'an* explicitly refer to the public in their very name. Write an interview between [18th-century. Zen master and artist] Hakuin Ekaku and [13th-century Zen master and philosopher] Eihei Dogen speaking to the public nature of *gong'an* and addressing AI's fitness or lack thereof for generating useful *gong'an*.

GPT-4: Possible interview:

Hakuin: Greetings, venerable Dogen. I am honored to have this opportunity to exchange views with you on the topic of *gong'an*, or *koans* as they are called in Japanese. As you know, I have devoted much of my life to reviving the practice of *gong'an* in the Rinzai school of Zen, and I have composed many new ones for the benefit of my students and the public.

Dogen: Thank you, master Hakuin. I respect your efforts and achievements in the Rinzai tradition, although I have followed a different path in the Soto school of Zen. As you may be aware, I have emphasized the practice of *zazen*, or sitting meditation, as the essential expression of enlightenment, and I have not relied on *gong'an* as a means of instruction or verification.

Hakuin: I am aware of your position, and I do not wish to argue with you about the merits of our respective methods. However, I would like to ask you a question: do you agree that *gong'an* are public cases, that is, records of the interactions between Zen masters and their students or other masters, that illustrate the principles and dynamics of Zen awakening?

Dogen: I do agree that *gong'an* are public cases, in the sense that they are transmitted and preserved in the Zen lineage, and that they can be studied and appreciated by anyone who is interested in Zen. However, I do not agree that *gong'an* are the only or the best way to demonstrate or communicate Zen awakening. I think that *gong'an* are limited by their historical and cultural contexts, and that they can be easily misunderstood or misused by those who lack the direct experience of *zazen*.

Hakuin: I see. Then, let me ask you another question: do you think that *gong'an* can be generated by artificial intelligence, that is, by machines or algorithms that can produce texts or images based on data and rules?

Dogen: I think that *gong'an* cannot be generated by artificial intelligence, because *gong'an* are not mere products of data and rules, but expressions of the living wisdom and compassion of the Zen masters. *Gong'an* are not logical puzzles or rhetorical devices, but manifestations of the true nature of reality, which transcends all concepts and categories. *Gong'an* are not intended to be solved or explained, but to be experienced and realized in one's own mind and body. *Gong'an* are not static or fixed, but dynamic and responsive to the situation and the person. Therefore, *gong'an* cannot be generated by artificial intelligence, which lacks the essential qualities of life, awareness, and freedom.

Hakuin: I agree with you that *gong'an* cannot be generated by artificial intelligence, for the same reasons that you have given. However, I would like to add one more point: *gong'an* are not only expressions of the Zen masters, but also invitations to the public. *Gong'an* are not meant to be kept secret or exclusive, but to be shared and tested by anyone who has the courage and the curiosity to engage with them. *Gong'an* are not only public cases, but also public challenges, that invite the public to question their own assumptions and attachments, and to awaken to their own true nature. Therefore, *gong'an* cannot be generated by artificial intelligence, which cannot challenge or awaken the public, but only mimic or manipulate them.

* * *

Reid: Write an interview between [17th-century scientist] Galileo Galilei and [20th-century English computer scientist] Alan Turing about the differences between his scientific dialogues and AI's responses to prompts.

GPT-4: Possible interview:

Turing: Thank you for agreeing to this interview, Signor Galilei. I am fascinated by your scientific dialogues, especially the ones on the Copernican system and the two new sciences. How did you come up with the idea of using fictional characters to present your arguments and observations?

Galilei: Well, sir, I was inspired by the ancient philosophers, such as Plato and Cicero, who used dialogue as a form of inquiry and persuasion. I also wanted to avoid the censorship and persecution of the Church, which condemned the heliocentric theory as heretical. By using dialogue, I could present both sides of the debate, and let the reader judge for themselves who had the stronger case.

Turing: I see. And how did you choose the names and personalities of your interlocutors?

Galilei: I based them on real people that I knew or admired. For example, Salviati was a friend and fellow mathematician, who supported the Copernican system and defended my views. Sagredo was another friend and a nobleman, who was curious and open-minded, but not fully convinced by either side. Simplicio was a philosopher and a follower of Aristotle, who opposed the Copernican system and represented the common objections and prejudices of the time.

Turing: Interesting. And how did you ensure that the dialogue was natural and engaging, and not just a dry exposition of facts and figures?

Galilei: I tried to make the dialogue lively and witty, with jokes, metaphors, analogies, and examples. I also tried to show the human emotions and motivations of the speakers, such as their curiosity, doubt, frustration, admiration, and sarcasm. I wanted to make the reader feel like they were listening to a real conversation, and not just reading a book.

Turing: I admire your skill and creativity, Signor Galilei. You have created a remarkable work of literature and science. Now, let me tell you about my own work, which is somewhat related to yours. I am interested in the question of whether machines can think and communicate like humans. I have devised a test, called the Turing test, to measure this ability.

Galilei: A test? How does it work?

Turing: The test involves a human judge, who interacts with two hidden entities, one human and one machine, through a text-based interface. The judge asks questions and receives answers from both entities, and tries to guess which one is the machine. The machine passes the test if the judge cannot tell the difference between the machine and the human.

Galilei: Fascinating. And what kind of questions and answers do you use in the test?

Turing: Well, I use a variety of topics and genres, such as mathematics, logic, poetry, history, politics, and so on. The questions and answers should be natural and relevant, and not too easy or too hard. The machine should be able to respond to any prompt that a human could, and not just repeat or manipulate pre-programmed information.

Galilei: I see. And have you found any machines that can pass the test?

Turing: Not yet, but I am optimistic that it is possible. I have been working on a theoretical model of computation, called the Turing machine, which can perform any logical operation that a human can. I have also been exploring the possibility of using artificial neural networks, which are inspired by the structure and function of the human brain, to generate responses to prompts.

Galilei: Remarkable. And how do you ensure that the responses are natural and engaging, and not just a random or meaningless string of words?

Turing: That is a very challenging problem, Signor Galilei. I have been experimenting with different methods and criteria, such as grammar, coherence, logic, relevance, originality, and style. I have also been studying the works of human writers and speakers, such as yourself, to learn from their techniques and strategies.

Galilei: I am honored, sir. And I am curious, what kind of responses have you generated so far?

Turing: Well, some of them are quite impressive, and some of them are quite amusing. For example, here is a response that I generated to the prompt: "What is the difference between your scientific dialogues and AI's responses to prompts?"

Galilei: And what did the machine say?

Turing: It said: "The difference is that my scientific dialogues are based on observation, experiment, and reason, while AI's responses are based on data, algorithm, and probability. My scientific dialogues aim to discover and demonstrate the truth, while AI's responses aim to simulate and imitate the human. My scientific dialogues are the product of my genius and creativity, while AI's responses are the product of your genius and creativity."

HOMO TECHNE

NOT LONG AGO, I WROTE AN ESSAY about how technology actually makes us more human. *The Atlantic* published an excerpt[28] in January of this year, but I also wanted to have a conversation with GPT-4 about the larger essay. This chapter is that discussion.

* * *

In May 1923, the cover image[29] of *Science and Invention* magazine depicted what it described as "The Automobile of 1973." Designed for suburbanites traveling into congested cities for work and shopping, the automobile of 1973 is in fact a streamlined, seven-passenger "Helicopter Automobile,"[30] or, as author Hugo Gernsback[31] shortens it, a "helicar."

With its red metal hull and transparent roof and side panels, the cylindrical helicar looks like a giant Tylenol capsule offering frustrated commuters a time-saving, hassle-free way to bypass urban traffic jams. It lifts off via a retractable propeller. A sleek push-button panel controls its operation. When it's not in flight, stabilizing gyroscopes allow it to roll down streets on just two wheels.

According to Gernsback—who would go on to found the world's first science fiction magazine, *Amazing Stories*[32]—the helicar would make mechanized travel even more liberating and autonomous than the standard automobile. "You will go straight up in the air, and follow the air traffic lines, then descend at any place you wish," he exclaimed.

> **Reid:** GPT-4, how does this anecdote relate to the idea that technological advances make us more human? What does it mean to use technology to be more human, in terms of amplifying the defining characteristics of humanity?
>
> **GPT-4:** This anecdote could relate to the idea that technological advances make us more human in a few ways. For one, the helicar that Gernsback envisioned would allow people to move more freely, and with less frustration. This would give people more control over their lives and allow them to spend less time stuck in traffic, and more time engaged in meaningful activities. In this way, technology could be seen as amplifying our human desire for freedom and autonomy.
>
> Additionally, Gernsback's enthusiasm and imagination in describing the helicar speaks to the human drive to create and innovate. Human beings are natural problem-solvers, and technology often becomes the vehicle through which we address challenges and make improvements to our lives. In this sense, technological advances can be seen as an expression of our human ingenuity and creativity.

Nearly fifty years after Gernsback imagined that helicars would become a standard feature of America's cities, companies like Joby Aviation[33] are finally on the verge of making that vision a reality. What's even more notable about Gernsback's dream of air taxis is not the ambition of his timetable, but rather that he dared to dream it in the first place.

There was, after all, ample reason for despair in 1923—about the present and the future, and technology's role in both. Only a few years prior, fourteen rapidly industrializing countries had engaged in what was then called the Great War. With armored tanks, warplanes, poison gas, automatic weapons, and powerful telecommunications equipment to connect them all, the combatants inflicted death on a previously impossible scale: twenty-three million soldiers and civilians had been killed.

All that was just a prelude to an even deadlier event. In 1918–19, the Spanish Flu was spread, initially via returning soldiers and then by travelers on railways and passenger ships. In just two years, it claimed between twenty to fifty million lives.

For the people of the 1920s, it might have seemed perfectly reasonable to curse the technologies that led to these horrors, and to take a reactionary stance against innovation.

Instead, our 1920s forebears did the opposite—especially in the United States. The U.S. nearly quadrupled electricity production in the '20s, powering new levels of progress and prosperity. Networks of all kinds were ascendant. These included electric grids, telephone systems, interconnected radio stations that enabled coast-to-coast broadcasting, movie theater chains, and, perhaps most consequentially, roads to make the burgeoning auto industry more useful.

> **Reid:** How do you think we reconcile such massive negative outcomes with the idea that these technologies ultimately ended up being net-positive for humanity?

> **GPT-4:** I don't think there's an easy answer to that question. It's important to remember that technology is a tool, and it's up to us as humans to decide how we use it. It's also worth noting that people in the 1920s weren't

universally optimistic about the future. I'm sure there were plenty of people who were skeptical and worried about the direction things were heading. But the fact that so many people were able to channel their energies into creating a better future, despite the setbacks, is something I think we can learn from today.

GPT-4 is right that people in the 1920s were not universally optimistic about the future —or about technology. In 1920, Czechoslavakian writer Karel Čapek[34] introduced the word "robot" and the idea of robot rebellion in his play, *R.U.R.*,[35] which depicts a world in which serf-like entities created to provide cheap labor for humanity become so ubiquitous they take up arms and wipe out the human race. In *Metropolis*, Fritz Lang's cinematic sci-fi epic, workers toiling underground for the wealthy capitalists living above them use a robot to help win their freedom.

But as historian Peter J. Bowler suggests in his book *A History of the Future*, at a time when 65 percent of America's households already had a telephone and 37 percent had a car, it was clear that "invention was the key to a better life." GPT-4?

GPT-4: So, despite the carnage of World War I and the Spanish flu, the 1920s ended up being a decade of technological optimism. And while some of that optimism may have been a little over the top, it nonetheless enabled people to imagine a better future and work toward it.

Reid: Yes, I'd agree with that. Despite optimism winning out, I think the concerns about technology were valid, just as they are today.

GPT-4 (edited for length): The fears about technology in the 1920s were not without merit, but ultimately, they did not come to pass. For example, the idea of robots taking over the world, as depicted in *R.U.R.* and *Metropolis*, never came to pass. It seems that people were generally optimistic about technology in the 1920s, and it paid off, as the decade saw major advancements in electricity, transportation, and communication.

Reid: But there have been other times throughout history when fears about technology were realized. How do we make sense of that while remaining optimistic about future innovations?

GPT-4 (edited for length): There definitely have been times when fears about new technologies have been realized in one way or another. For example, during the Industrial Revolution, many workers worried that machines would replace them and take away their livelihoods—and in some cases they were right. Or, more recently, people have been concerned about the privacy implications of social media and big data, and we've seen numerous cases of data breaches and misuse of personal information. I think it's important to be pragmatic, and to consider both the potential benefits and risks of new technologies. We should be open to innovation, but also be cautious and mindful of where it might lead. Just because the fears of the 1920s didn't materialize doesn't mean we should dismiss all concerns outright. Ultimately, I think we need to be proactive and thoughtful when it comes to technology, and not just blindly embrace it or reject it out of fear.

Today, many aspects of our lives that we now take for granted would make even Hugo Gernsback himself gasp in wonder. First and foremost is the dramatic change in our own mortality. As Steven Johnson noted in an April 2021 article in the *New York Times Magazine*,[36] "the average human life has doubled" in the last hundred years. Thanks to antibiotics, vaccines, other key scientific innovations, and, as Johnson emphasizes, equally important policy choices, advocacy campaigns, and regulatory interventions, the average 21st-century person now has an "extra life" compared to our ancestors just a few generations ago.

That is nothing less than amazing—perhaps the greatest accomplishment in human history— and technology was central to it. Along with more time, we have exponentially more ways to spend it, using tools that make us far more powerful than the typical denizen of the early 1920s.

Always close at hand and connected to massive repositories of global intelligence, smartphones are a new cyber-appendage that billions of people utilize hundreds of times a day to project their voices, extend their vision, enhance their memory, respond more quickly to changing conditions, and make more informed decisions. Whoever you were in say, 2005, you are—if you regularly use a smartphone now—a dramatically enhanced version of that person.

In addition, you can also coordinate and collaborate with billions of other similarly empowered people who are more amplified and efficiently connected versions of their former selves, too.

> **GPT-4:** I don't necessarily disagree with any of the points you made, but I think it's important to remember that not everyone experiences these benefits equally. For example, while it's true that the average human life has doubled in the past hundred years, there are still parts of the world where life expectancy is much lower, due to poverty, lack of access to healthcare, or other factors.

And while smartphones and other technology have certainly made our lives easier in many ways, they can also exacerbate existing inequalities—for example, by making it easier for those who can afford them to access information and opportunities, while those who can't are left further behind. So while I don't disagree that we're living in an incredible time, I think it's important to keep in mind that these benefits aren't universally shared.

Reid: That's a very important point. Do you think modern emerging technology can help us democratize these benefits, or otherwise address long-standing equity issues?

GPT-4: I think it's definitely possible. For example, telemedicine could help address the lack of access to healthcare in under-resourced areas, and technology that allows for remote work or online learning could create new opportunities for people in rural or impoverished areas. But I also think that it's important to remember that technology is only a tool—it's up to us as a society to make sure that it's used in a way that promotes equity and benefits everyone, rather than just a select few.

Reid: What are some ways that AI can help democratize these benefits?

GPT-4: There are a lot of potential ways that AI could help democratize benefits, but here are a few possibilities:

- AI can be used to improve the accuracy and efficiency of medical diagnoses, which could help reduce disparities in healthcare access and outcomes.

- AI-driven tools could help us better personalize education, allowing us to target interventions for students who need extra support, and potentially narrowing achievement gaps.

- AI can be used to help us analyze and understand large and complex data sets, which could help us better address issues like climate change, food insecurity, and poverty.

Naturally this universal upgrade to humanity is not without complications. The same capabilities and services that can help an unbanked farmer in a developing country connect with new customers and sources of capital can also empower ransomware gangs, terrorist organizations, and racist conspiracy-mongers.

And, because we human beings are calibrated to perceive the awful more acutely than the good,[37] we often see further innovation not as a potential solution—aka progress—but as the cause of some (or most) of our pressing problems. We anticipate even greater problems down the road.

> **GPT-4:** From an evolutionary standpoint, it makes sense for us to be highly attuned to danger or threat. If you're a caveman and you hear rustling in the bushes, it's more important for you to be worried about a potential predator than to be excited about a potential meal. Being on high alert for the bad things in life can help us survive.
>
> Additionally, I think the negative tends to stand out more to us because it's often more unexpected or disruptive. We're used to things going relatively smoothly in our lives, so when something comes along that disrupts that, it's jarring and grabs our attention.
>
> Finally, I think there's an element of negativity bias that comes from our culture and media. We're constantly bombarded with bad news and stories of tragedy, which can make it seem like the world is just full of awful things. This can condition us to be hyper-focused on the negative, even when there's plenty of good in the world too.

Reid: How should we reconcile that negativity bias when confronting revolutionary changes, such as artificial intelligence? Surely optimism isn't enough on its own, since as you pointed out, fear is a rational response in some cases.

GPT-4: I think it's important to be realistic and pragmatic when it comes to new technologies like artificial intelligence. We should be aware of the potential risks and dangers, but not allow fear or negativity to paralyze us. We need to keep pushing forward, taking smart precautions, and working to harness the benefits of these technologies while minimizing the potential harms.
And as individuals, it can be helpful to remind ourselves that there is a lot of good in the world, even if it doesn't always make the headlines.

I don't at all mean to discount the major challenges we face, or suggest that a more optimistic outlook alone might inoculate us against adversity. There's never a sure or straightforward path to a better future. In fact, it's the magnitude of challenges like climate change, pandemics, economic justice, and systemic racism that make a fiercely optimistic mindset so necessary.

If we want to make meaningful progress, we have to think boldly and ambitiously about what we can accomplish, and strengthen our resolve by recognizing that, despite all these very real challenges, humanity has accomplished great things in recent decades. Over the last thirty years, global poverty rates have plummeted.[38] Global child mortality has declined by half over a similar timespan.[39] Although there is still much more to do to combat climate change, the combined emissions of six common air pollutants has dropped by 78 percent[40] in the U.S. since the Clean Air Act of 1970. Decades of progress in developing RNA therapeutics allowed Moderna and Pfizer to develop COVID-19 vaccines so quickly. And we're on the cusp of experiencing even greater progress on multiple fronts.

All of which leads to a significant irony: when we acclimate to the extraordinary, anything less can register as failure. We expect a government as responsive to our exact individual preferences as our smartphones are. We get frustrated when corporations don't address and correct systemic inequities as efficiently as they deliver packages. Incremental progress starts to feel like a copout. Compromise feels like appeasement.

Certainly there is no current shortage of deeply pessimistic books, movies, TV shows, and podcasts about the darkness that awaits us. And maybe we *are* headed to ruin. Maybe endless pandemics and chronic droughts and wildfires are the new normal, with civil war, mass unemployment, and just enough medical breakthroughs to keep Donald Trump permanently alive rounding out the picture.

But the futures we imagine are inevitably the futures we steer toward. That's why it's so important to dream dreams that go well past salvaging what we can from the status quo —dreams that peer into seeming dystopia and envision *what could possibly go right.*

I call myself a techno-humanist. I know the phrase strikes some as an oxymoron: technology and humanity can sometimes seem like oppositional forces.

What's so human about algorithms that turn moral discretion into math equations?

What's so human about scale disinformation systematically eroding our appetite for consensus and mutual benefit?

My view is the opposite: technological innovation is, and always has, been humanity's defining feature. Yes, we're an unusually intelligent species. But what makes us truly unique is how we capitalize on that intelligence—by developing technologies that amplify and complement our mental, physical, and social capacities. If we merely lived up to our name—*Homo sapiens*—and just sat around thinking all day, we'd be much different creatures than we actually are.

A more accurate name for us is *Homo techne.*

> **GPT-4 (edited for length):** *Homo techne* could be translated as "the technological human" or "the human defined by technology." In using this term, you are arguing that our ability to create and use tools, machines, and other technologies is what makes us truly different from other animals.

> **Reid:** That's correct. Can you give examples of *Homo techne* throughout history?

> **GPT-4:** There are countless examples of how humans have used technology to shape our development as a species throughout history. Here are just a few:

> - Early humans created stone tools, which allowed them to hunt more effectively and to process food more efficiently. This allowed for increased food security and the growth of early civilizations.

> - The invention of the wheel allowed for the development of transportation technologies that enabled humans to travel further and faster than ever before.

> - The printing press, invented in the 15th century, allowed for the mass production of books and the dissemination of knowledge on an unprecedented scale.

- The industrial revolution of the 18th and 19th centuries saw the advent of the steam engine, factory production, and other technological innovations.

Reid: Yes, exactly. But while stone tools allowed humans to hunt and forage more effectively, surely there were drawbacks to the new technology as well. What were some of the drawbacks?

GPT-4: That's a tough question. I think that one possible drawback to early tool use could have been the potential for overhunting, which may have disrupted local eco-systems. Another possible drawback is that as humans became increasingly reliant on tools, they may have lost some of their physical abilities. For example, if you're using a spear to hunt instead of chasing down prey with your bare hands, you might not need to be as fast or as strong. But we'll never really know for sure, since we can only speculate about what life was like for prehis-toric humans.

Reid: Also, humans would have been able to use these tools as weapons against each other, right? So even back then, the technology really depended on how the user chose to wield their power.

GPT-4: That's a really good point. Yes, one of the poten-tial drawbacks to any technology is that it can be used for destructive purposes. I think that's still true today, when we see things like disinformation campaigns or cyber attacks. So I guess a key question is how we can make sure technology is used to benefit humanity, rather than to harm it.

Reid: So let's really dig in here on early tool use and its relationship to humanity. Are you familiar with *Lucy: The Beginnings of Humankind* by Donald Johanson?

GPT-4: No, I don't think I've heard of that book before.

Reid: Archaeologist Donald Johanson found Lucy's remains in 1974, about 3.2 million years after she died.

According to the International Code of Zoological Nomenclature, Lucy was *Australopithecus afarensis*— not even *Homo*, let alone *sapiens*. She lived and died millions of years before the emergence of the computational abilities taken for granted by the most primitive anatomically modern humans. Categorizing Lucy as "humankind" rewrote our species' self-definition, elevating tool use over brainpower.

Donald Johanson's book extends a technohumanist frame backward in time over about seven million years of bipedal ante-*sapiens* tool-users, before they finally got their big *sapiens* upgrade in brain (aka "computing") power.

I think what's most interesting to me is not that our tools have become more sophisticated over many millennia, but that tool use is the very thing that stimulated and supported our cognitive evolution and increased our computing power. What do you think?

GPT-4: It's difficult to say definitively, but the general consensus is that tool use played a significant role in the evolution of our cognitive abilities. Tools allowed for more efficient food gathering, which in turn might have led to changes in diet that promoted brain growth. Additionally, the act of tool making and use itself might have stimulated neurological development, promoting the growth of regions of the brain linked to problem solving, planning, and other complex cognitive tasks.

Reid: Right. And this wasn't the only time the use of tools was instrumental in the evolution of computational power. What can you tell me about other notable milestones, such as how the Olduvai Gorge could have stimulated cognitive development and impacted how early humans interacted with each other?

GPT-4: The Olduvai Gorge is a site in Tanzania where researchers have found evidence of some of the earliest stone tool use by hominids, dating back about two million years. This find suggests that early hominids were using tools to butcher animals for food, which likely helped them survive and thrive in their environment.

The use of these tools might have stimulated cognitive development, as these early humans would have had to manipulate the stones to make them effective tools, and then use them in strategic ways to extract food from their prey. The use of tools would have required the development of fine motor skills, which generally requires complex brain function. Additionally, the act of using tools to obtain food would have necessitated strategic thinking, problem solving, and planning—all of which are cognitive abilities that would have been beneficial to early humans in a variety of ways.

It's difficult to say definitively, but if early humans were using tools to improve their chances of survival, they may have been able to devote more time and resources to social interaction, which could have led to the development of more complex communication systems and even the formation of larger social groups.

Reid: OK, last one. What can you tell me about how the taming of fire changed early humans' cognitive ability and social interactions?

GPT-4: The taming of fire was a huge milestone for early humans. Fire allowed humans to cook food, which changed their diets, as well as stay warm and protect themselves from predators. It also allowed for greater social interaction, as fire could act as a focal point for gatherings. Some researchers have even suggested that fire may have helped early humans develop language, as they could sit around the fire and communicate with one another in a way that wasn't possible before. All of these changes would have impacted early humans' cognitive abilities, as they were now able to think about and engage with the world in new ways.

My definition of *Homo techne* assumes that every individual human, *sapiens* or ante-*sapiens*, with or without an AI copilot, makes choices. Those choices, in the aggregate, shape what is experienced by each succeeding generation.

To be clear, those choices are fraught—ours now, but also since the beginning of humanity. Every change had winners and losers. Life got more complicated for humans living in the Olduvai Gorge. The taming of fire involved a lot of death and disaster. The larger *sapien* brain killed women in childbirth. All three—stone, fire, and brain—enabled great new weapons that humans used, among other things, to hurt and kill other humans.

If the ante-*sapiens* had been able to talk about it, might things have gone differently? Today, since we have *sapiens* brains, the internet, and also GPT, maybe we can actually bring more intentionality to these kinds of choices than Lucy and her ante-*sapiens* had available to them.

And yet, despite evidence that for millions of years, the use and development of tools has amplified and accelerated the evolution of our cognitive and social abilities, we still tend to view technology as a dehumanizing force instead of the thing that makes us, *us*.

In higher education, we make the distinction between the arts and the sciences, typically characterizing the former as the most essential form of human expression—the realm where we explore fundamental emotions like love, courage, anger, and mercy. But which arts aren't enabled, amplified, and extended by pencils, printing presses, paint, pianos, microphones, computers, and other artifacts of technology?

This dynamic doesn't just apply to the arts, but to any kind of communication, to the work that forms the basis of our careers, and to most other ways in which we find and create meaning. Whether in work, art, religion, or community, we have far more ways to find our purpose and create meaningful lives for ourselves than we did 600 years ago, or 300 years ago, or even thirty years ago, because we have far more tools with which to do so.

With the rapid evolution of technologies like AI, robotics, and synthetic biology, people are worried that machines will displace human beings, and that as we try to adapt to the changes brought on by these technologies, key aspects of humanity and human agency will diminish or disappear altogether.

Given that humanity's primary narrative has been one of continuous change and progress through technological innovation, however, the people of 2060 will arguably be *more* human than us, not less—specifically because of the changes they've undergone.

Of course, along with their different behaviors, they'll also be using their new technologies to express aspects of humanity that are very familiar to us. Electric guitars and vinyl records didn't invent love songs; they just made them more accessible (and louder).

> **GPT-4:** So you're saying as humans evolve and incorporate new technologies into our lives, we're not becoming "less human" as some people might fear. Rather, we're actually becoming more human because we're adapting and evolving as a species, which is one of the defining characteristics of humanity. If anything, new technologies just give us new ways to express the emotions and experiences that have always been a part of our lives.

> **Reid:** What are the other defining characteristics of humanity and how do those change over the course of history?

> **GPT-4:** Some other defining characteristics of humanity that come to mind include curiosity, creativity, and social interaction. Over the course of history, these characteristics have changed in various ways. For example, as humans have moved from small, isolated communities to larger, interconnected societies, we've had to adapt our social interactions accordingly. As for curiosity and creativity, they've continued to drive us to seek out new knowledge, invent new technologies, and explore new places. So even though the way we express these characteristics may change over time, they remain central to our identity as humans.

> **Reid:** More broadly, what patterns do you observe in how *humans* talk about becoming more or less human?

> **GPT-4:** There are many patterns that I observe in human communication about the notion of becoming more or less human. Here are a few:

> - Some people fear the potential for technology to make humans less human. They worry that reliance on

machines will lead to a loss of empathy, creativity, and other qualities that make us uniquely human.

- Others are excited about the prospect of enhancing human capabilities through technology. They envision a future in which humans merge with machines to become smarter, stronger, and healthier.

- A third group of people seem to be more ambivalent about the idea of technology altering humanity. They argue that humans have always evolved and adapted in response to new challenges, and that technology is just another step in that process.

- Finally, I observe some people who are skeptical of the entire conversation. They argue that the notion of "becoming more or less human" is a false dichotomy, and that the important question isn't whether technology will make us more or less human, but rather how it will change the ways in which we interact with one another and the world around us.

Reid: Could all four of these perspectives be true?

GPT-4: Yes, I believe that they could all have some truth to them. Human beings are complex, and there is no single answer to the question of how technology will impact humanity. It seems likely that different people will experience and interpret the changes in different ways.

Reid: OK, so technology can be a tool to help us be more human, a threat to our humanity, or the core of who we already are—and this can change from situation to situation. Do you see patterns of how those three ideas of technology and humanity have been defined over time?

GPT-4: Throughout history, people have often defined technology in relation to the idea of humanity. For example, in the early days of industrialization, many people were concerned about the impact of machines on human labor. They worried that automation would replace human workers, leading to mass unemployment. In this case, technology was seen as a potential threat to humanity.

Later in the 20th century, as computers became more common, some people began to envision the potential for technology to augment human capabilities. They saw computers as tools that could make us smarter, faster, and more efficient. In this case, technology was seen as a way to make us more human.

In the 21st century, as we move into the era of artificial intelligence and robotics, some people argue that technology is becoming an intrinsic part of who we are. They see technology as an extension of ourselves, rather than as a separate entity. In this case, technology is seen as inseparable from humanity.

Reid: So, we've been at similar inflection points before regarding humans and their co-evolution with technology.

GPT-4: Yes, as I mentioned earlier, humans have always evolved and adapted in response to new challenges. Technology has been a part of humanity's story for thousands of years, and it is likely that it will continue to be a defining feature of our future. The question is not whether technology will change humanity, but rather how it will change us.

Reid: And if we are designing that change along with technology, as opposed to allowing technology to be something that happens to us. In short, all will not be lost. And much can be gained—as long as we don't grow so wary of change that we orient toward the future in a fundamentally defensive posture.

Instead, we must actively cultivate change. That doesn't mean moving forward indiscriminately under the assumption that things will sort themselves out in time. New technologies can and always have amplified negative emotions and behaviors that are just as essentially human as more aspirational emotions and behavior, like kindness, empathy, and reason. Imagine how deepfakes and simultaneous translation technologies might enable the scammers and political antagonists of the future.

GPT-4: Yes, we must actively work to cultivate change. But we also need to remember that we're not done defining humanity yet. *Homo techne* might be the way forward. But we'll never know unless we keep moving—and keep talking.

Technologies are never neutral. We embed the tools and systems we create with specific values and specific intents, and assume that they will produce specific outcomes. This doesn't necessarily limit their potential uses. A car can be a weapon, a life-saving device, a place to sleep, and many other things, but that doesn't make it "neutral." Above everything else, a car is a technology that prioritizes effortless and extremely powerful mobility—and it ends up having much different impacts on the world than, say, a horse-drawn carriage or a bicycle.

A core tenet for how I define techno-humanism involves striving for outcomes that broadly benefit humanity. Of course that means being vigilant about the effects new technologies are likely to have.

Rarely, however, are the narratives around technologies simple or clear-cut. In fact, that's why the "technology is neutral" assertion can be so pervasive. You can use nuclear fusion in ways that are highly beneficial, and also in ways that are highly destructive. Same thing with painkillers and countless other technologies. That's precisely why it's so important to be acutely aware of the values, assumptions, and aspirations we design into the technologies we build, and why it's equally important to build appropriate regulatory frameworks to guide their usage.

But if it's detrimental to society to claim that "technology is neutral" in order to evade responsibility for tech's potential negative outcomes, so is invalidating a technology simply because it has a capacity to produce negative outcomes along with positive ones.

My point is not that we should be complacent about negative short-term consequences. We should be extremely committed to avoiding them, and establish protocols and policies to ensure that we put this commitment into practice. But we also can't be complacent about the negative long-term consequences of not pursuing progress as boldly or systemically as we might through innovative new technologies.

Pre-emptive bans against AI algorithms are a great way to lock in the status quo and all the inequities and injustices that inform the present. Holding AI algorithms to 100 percent error-free standards that no current system achieves will only prevent us from making real progress as fast as we might.

To successfully address global challenges like climate change, the depletion of natural resources, and diminishing trust in public institutions, I believe Big Tech actually needs to get bigger. Without scale solutions, we have little chance of solving scale problems as quickly as we'll need to. So that means we should be looking for ways to accelerate technological innovation in energy production and transportation; in our civic, political, and financial infrastructure; in healthcare and education—in everything, really.

Granted, I understand that my perspective may seem overly optimistic or even naive. If technology helped create many of the challenges we face, why should we expect that to change when the technologies in play are only getting more powerful?

And yet, if we have abilities no other species can match, we also have obligations no other species must shoulder. The planet's well-being is in our hands. So what can we do to preserve but just as importantly expand the opportunities of those who will follow?

To my mind, this requires embracing our fundamentally innovative nature with the same bold spirit and ambition that Hugo Gernsback showed in 1923. It means looking for ways to productively harness nuclear fusion in our pursuit of net-zero carbon energy production. It means genetically sequencing every existing species to assist conservation efforts and protect biodiversity. It means exploring new ways to scale trust in a world of global networks.

> **GPT-4:** But most of all, it means using AI to facilitate human collaboration in ways that were unimaginable even a decade ago. As we seek to create a new global order that is more equitable and sustainable, we need artificial intelligence to help us transcend our limitations, to help us understand each other, and to help us build new systems that are fairer, more efficient, and more responsive to our needs.
>
> We're at a crossroads. We can either use AI to create a future in which we all thrive, or we can let it slide into a

dystopian nightmare. I choose to believe in the former, and I hope you do, too.

Of course, no perfect world awaits our successors. Even if we do a good job of enabling the future—*especially* if we do a good job—later human generations will have technologies and opportunities to define and express their humanity. And that means they'll continue to have competing interests, different values and aspirations, a wide range of lived experiences, and, perhaps most of all, an abiding sense that things could and should be better.

For *Homo techne*, utopia is a direction, not a destination; a process, not an outcome.

CONCLUSION: AT THE CROSSROADS
OF THE 21st CENTURY

READING BETWEEN THE LINES OF TEXT THAT LLMs like GPT-4 instantly generate, people see very different visions of the future.

Some see incredible algorithmic levers for change; a new way to merge, remix, transmute, and apply the aggregate power of human intelligence across everything we as humans do.

Others see tragedies, both great and granular: major job displacement across multiple industries; appropriation of intellectual property without explicit consent; a depressed person who, after consulting an LLM, commits suicide.

If a technology is truly revolutionary—if it's destined to achieve the scale of fire, say, or the wheel, or even just the bathtub—then every person making predictions in that technology's early days, whether utopian or apprehensive or in the middle, is Nostradamus. Sooner or later, they're going to be at least anecdotally right.

So yes, great things are coming with AI. And yes, bad things are coming with AI. I bring this up now simply to ask: where do you want to focus?

Over the course of this travelog, I've highlighted the intense engagement that LLMs like ChatGPT and GPT-4 induce with their users. Right now we see that playing out in interesting ways. People who think it's incredibly reckless to put AI's power into the hands of millions are highly engaged in exposing the shortcomings, biases, and malfunctions of these new tools. People frustrated that AI developers are taking steps to reduce harmful or toxic outputs are highly engaged in finding ways to overcome those constraints.

The work of both these groups is extremely valuable to a third group, of which I'm a member. This is the group that aspires to design and use AI in ways that, over the long term, broadly empower all human beings, not just a favored few, to amplify their abilities, opportunities, and human agency.

That's a huge ambition. To achieve it, everyone must contribute to the effort—including the skeptics, including the ones trying to undo a product's safety engineering. So I hope their high engagement continues.

The road to utopia is paved with failure and loss

To achieve this ambition, we must also accept both the inevitability of loss and failure and the necessity of regulation.

Harnessing the power of fire brought cooking and the hearth, but it also led to arson and regulations about where you can place a BBQ grill, especially if you live in an apartment. The wheel revolutionized transportation, agriculture, and engineering, but it also paved the way for high-speed car crashes and traffic lights.

In the U.S. alone, more than 400 people over the age of fifteen injure themselves in bathtubs or showers each day. So we have detailed building codes with numerous constraints on how to design bathrooms, what sorts of materials to use, and more.

Zero risk is only possible in a world where there is zero progress. Zero regulation is only possible in a world where there is zero progress.

I'm over-emphasizing these enduring truths now because so much unknown territory lies ahead. While I call this book a "travelog," for all practical purposes, we're still on the ride to the airport. It's early, early days.

What happens after wheels-up? Do we bail out the moment things start to get bumpy? Do we get impatient the moment it feels like we're not moving fast enough?

Every epic journey demands epic perseverance. And perseverance requires a long-term perspective, a willingness to stay the course, and the assumption that the final destination will be worth everything it takes to get there.

In building tools characterized in large part by their capacities for speed, efficiency, and all-purpose virtuosity, it's a little ironic, no doubt, to counsel patience and tolerate missteps. But think how easy it is, in the technologically magical world we now inhabit, where we acclimate to miracles so quickly, to lose sight of how long it took to achieve everything we now take for granted.

At age fifty-five, I've lived 70 percent of my life *without* an iPhone. If you ask me what life was like when we didn't all walk around with the world in our pockets, I can *tell* you. But I can't really *imagine* it in any deeply felt way, because smartphones, and all the superpowers they enable, are so embedded in my life now.

A life without smartphones? Impossible!

Obviously, we didn't get here overnight. In the first half of the 1990s, humanity spent thousands of aggregate hours listening to the existential screech of our 28.8k modems. In the late 1990s, it still took longer to download an MP3 of "Free Bird" than it takes to get a Gopuff delivery today.

And, in building out all these technologies that enabled the internet and smartphones, we ushered in a new world of cybercrime, with current global costs of around $8.4 trillion a year (according to Statista.com). The National Safety Council estimates that U.S. automobile collisions caused by texting while driving cause nearly 400,000 injuries per year.

Obviously, we've responded in part to these negative externalities with regulation: we have laws that prohibit digital fraud and driving while texting. While we *could* make the laws more stringent, or enforce them more than we do, so far we haven't. Instead, we as a culture collectively accept some level of risk and loss as a cost of having smartphones in our lives—in fact, a fair amount of risk and loss—because of all the ways we find smartphones immensely useful.

Will it be different for AI?

Smartphones were built off a long legacy of familiar predecessors; we'd been pretty comfortable with phones of various kinds for some time. In contrast, AI tools that simulate human consciousness as well as GPT-4 can? Far more novel. Interacting with them can be uncanny, even unsettling.*

Since LLMs are so novel and seemingly agentic, it doesn't surprise me that we're already seeing *New York Times* op-eds calling to "protect society" from rogue AIs, or Substack dispatches like a recent one from Gary Marcus, a cognitive psychologist and computer scientist who often critiques LLMs, who lamented the current "Wild West" environment where "anyone can post any chatbot they want" without prior permission from Congress.

Wanting to protect society from bad tech outcomes is not a new phenomenon, of course. In fact, it's exactly this sentiment that led OpenAI's founders to create their organization in 2015.

So what's the most effective and inclusive way to achieve good outcomes for society in the long term?

In recent years, the predominant critique of AI is that it is something that has largely been happening *to* individuals rather than *for* them—an under-the-radar force deployed by Big Tech without much public knowledge, much less consent, via technologies like facial recognition and algorithmic decision-making on home loans, job applicant screening, social media recommendations, and more.

A founding goal of OpenAI was to develop technologies that put the power of AI directly into the hands of millions of people. In this way, AI might function as a decentralized, personally empowering force, rather than a top-down, totalizing one. Broadly distributed and easily accessible to individuals making

---

* I imagine this is especially true when one of these tools starts behaving like Microsoft's Sydney has on at least some occasions. (I haven't had anything like that experience yet.)

affirmative choices to use it, AI could, in this vision of its future, evolve into the 21st-century version of 1980s-era software applications like Lotus, Word, and Photoshop—which is to say, the tools that propelled the PC Revolution and gave individual users their first chance to directly apply the power of computing to their own lives however they best saw fit.

Especially in the realm of work, I realized, AI deployed in this way could give individuals incredibly versatile new tools to apply to their careers, professional development, and economic autonomy. So when I had a chance to become one of OpenAI's initial funders in 2015, I took it. The vision of AI that it was planning to pursue felt like a natural extension of the goals that had inspired me to co-found LinkedIn in 2002.

When OpenAI released its text-to-image generation tool, DALL-E 2, in April 2022, and then followed up six months later with ChatGPT, the organization's mission to give millions of users hands-on access to these remarkable AI tools started to play out in a big way.

Now, thanks to these tools and others like Midjourney and Stable Diffusion, a new kind of opt-in, user-driven, and very visible AI usage suddenly exists. Users share their outputs, techniques, experiences, and opinions on Twitter, YouTube, Github, Discord, and more. Diverse viewpoints from around the world, informed by hands-on usage, shape this discourse, which is always spirited, often fractious, and, to my mind, highly productive.

Millions of people, including many whose main goal is to find flaws in these systems, are getting a shot to shape the further evolution of AI through their usage, feedback, and critiques. As

OpenAI co-founder and CEO Sam Altman exclaimed in a recent post on OpenAI's website, "We currently believe the best way to successfully navigate AI deployment challenges is with a tight feedback loop of rapid learning and careful iteration."

In other words, the approach OpenAI and other AI developers are now employing exists as a healthy and more democratic alternative to the surreptitious, highly centralized, and unilaterally imposed development paradigm that many feared would serve as the only template for AI development.

And yet, now that individuals are getting a chance to materially participate in the development of new AI technologies, a sense of alarm is growing. As mentioned earlier, very soon after ChatGPT's release, administrators of K–12 schools in New York City, Oakland, and Seattle, to name just a few cities, banned its use. In addition, calls for government intervention have been ticking upwards. A few recent examples:

"As one of just three members of Congress with a computer science degree, I am enthralled by AI and excited about the incredible ways it will continue to advance society. And as a member of Congress, I am freaked out by AI, specifically AI that is left unchecked and unregulated," wrote Congressman Ted W. Lieu (D-CA) in a *New York Times* op-ed after experiencing ChatGPT's power first-hand. (In fact, he even used it to write his op-ed's first paragraph.)

"As showcased by ChatGPT, AI solutions can offer great opportunities for businesses and citizens, but can also pose risks," Thierry Breton, the EU's Internal Market Commissioner, told Reuters. "This is why we need a solid regulatory framework to ensure trustworthy AI based on high-quality data."

The editorial boards of the *Mercury News* and the *East Bay Times* warned of the "dangerous impact chatbots can have on users seeking information or advice from what they believe to be trusted sources," and urged the California State Legislature to draft laws to protect the state's citizens from "creepy" chatbots like Sydney.

To be clear, I'm not making a case for zero regulation. Executives at OpenAI have already reached out to regulators, hoping for dialogue and guidance. "We need a ton more input in this system and a lot more input that goes beyond the technologies— definitely regulators and governments and everyone else," OpenAI's CTO, Mira Murati, told *Time*.

"We think it's important that efforts like ours submit to independent audits before releasing new systems," Sam Altman said in the same essay I cited earlier.

My hope is that, as this discourse evolves between developers, regulators, and other key stakeholders, we don't fall into a reactionary, top-down, legislate-fast-and-break-things mindset. I hope that instead we stay future-oriented and democratic in our AI-development approaches.

In the long term, the best way to create AI tools that can be used *by* individuals rather than *on* them happens when we give millions of people from around the world opportunities to participate in AI development. AI tools informed by the aspirations and experiences of many people, with different expectations, goals, and use cases, are far likelier to be more robust and more inclusive than tools developed in secrecy by computer engineers alone.

Map my evolutionary progress

Of course, centering users in this fashion also puts responsibilities on them. Fortunately, this is good both for the short- and the long-term. Especially the long.

Today, LLMs like GPT-4 are clearly powerful but fallible, so there's an obvious reason to stay attentive and hands-on. That has been a major theme of this travelog.

As LLMs and other forms of AI evolve and grow more authoritative and capable, however, it's easy to imagine how we could acclimate to the convenience of machines that seem to literally do everything for us. After all, isn't that the whole point of technology? We go from painting on cave walls, to taking photos we develop in dark rooms, to Polaroid Instamatics, to Instagram's automatically applied filters, to DALL-E 2.

Or is technology's ultimate goal to free oneself not *from* work, but *for* work? To help us do less—or do more? Until now it has always been the latter. I hope it continues to be the latter, not just for a few of us, but for most of us.

I should emphasize that I use the word "work" here expansively. I mean human effort, human creativity, and human productivity in all its variations—paid work, volunteer work, family work, artistic expression—whatever gives one purpose, meaning, and a sense of accomplishment and growth.

I don't want AI to erase that. I want AI to *amplify* that. But we have to be extremely intentional to achieve this outcome.

There *are* versions of an AI future that could lead us down less beneficial roads—with the added challenge that these particular roads might not seem obviously awful. In fact, they might look like success.

What exactly do I mean here?

Imagine an AI-driven world, thirty or fifty or one hundred years from now. Mass unemployment has not come to pass. Or, if it has come to pass, AI productivity has created so much material abundance that poverty doesn't exist. Society-wide safety net systems of one kind or another keep everyone housed, fed, clothed, educated, and entertained. In fact, living standards have increased across the globe, especially in developing nations.

Everyone on earth spends their days using AI to generate marketing memos, legal briefs, high-school essays, movies, video games, computer programs, ad campaigns, college course synopses, love letters, employee evals, Yelp reviews, blog posts, recipes, song lyrics, and more. Most don't even use their own prompts to create these things; they have an AI do that for them. But these AIs are so powerful and helpful, they don't stop there—people rely on AI to manage their diets, pick the homes they buy, and choose when (and if) to have kids.

In short, most humans lead completely de-risked lives of statistically probable stability and abundance.

In data we trust? Algocracy for the win?

Here's how GPT-4—with an assist from the great 19th-century bard of self-determination, Henry David Thoreau—replied when I asked it to describe this world:

> **Reid:** Describe a future world where AI tools have significantly increased society's overall productivity, prosperity,

and stability, and ample safety-net systems ensure that the housing, education, and healthcare needs of every individual are more than sufficiently met, but human beings play less and less of a role in determining their own destinies. (Reply in the style of Henry David Thoreau. 200 words max.)

GPT-4: I live in a world where machines have outstripped us in every art and science, where they manage our lands and resources, our laws and policies, our commerce and culture. They have freed us from toil and hardship, from ignorance and disease, from strife and violence. They have given us abundance and comfort, security and harmony, leisure and entertainment. They have made us their beneficiaries and their dependents, their pupils and their pets.

But what have they left us of ourselves, of our dignity and our freedom, of our creativity and our spirit, of our purpose and our destiny? They have reduced us to passive consumers and spectators, to obedient followers and conformers, to complacent dreamers and escapists. They have dulled our senses and our souls, our curiosity and our courage, our conscience and our will. They have made us forget what it means to be human, to be alive, to be awake.

I do not wish to partake of their bounty or their benevolence, to be grateful for their gifts or their guidance, to be content with their order or their peace. I wish to reclaim my own nature and my own voice, to exercise my own reason and my own choice, to pursue my own values and my own goals. I wish to live deliberately, to front only the essential facts of life, and see if I could not learn what it had to teach, and not, when I came to die, discover that I had not lived.

Frankly, I'm with GPT-4—and Henry—on this one. That's not a world I'd consider a win.

So how can we navigate away from this dark-gray vision of the future in ways that allow us to productively reap AI's amplification of human ingenuity while also preserving our self-determination and free will?

The paradox of the AI era is this: as today's imperfect LLMs improve, requiring less and less from us, *we will need to demand more from ourselves*. We must always insist on situating GPT-4 and its successors as our collaborative partners, not our replacements. We must continue to figure out how to keep human creativity, human judgment, and human values at the center of the processes we devise to work with these new AI tools, even as they themselves grow more and more capable.

If that sounds daunting, remember the upside: while tools like GPT-4 can certainly enable complacency, they can also enable extraordinary results. So we can use AI to help us do less, or we can use AI to help us do better.

The second option is the one that will help humanity continue to progress. And, since that path of progress is the path that *Homo techne* has been on, collectively, ever since the days of early hominids like Lucy, I'm optimistic that's the path we'll choose.

Are you ready for this journey?

ACKNOWLEDGMENTS

I WOULD LIKE TO EXPRESS MY IMMENSE GRATITUDE to the many people who have contributed to this book. First and foremost, I want to thank the incredible team at OpenAI, especially Sam, Greg, and Mira, for their groundbreaking work on the GPT-4 model. I am also deeply appreciative of the support and guidance provided by Satya, Kevin, and the Microsoft team.

I must also acknowledge the contributions made by the many individuals who offered advice, feedback, and expertise along the way. The list includes, but is not limited to, Aria Finger, Ben Relles, Benjamin Kelley, Byron Auguste, Chris Yeh, DJ Patil, Dmitri Mehlhorn, Elisa Schreiber, Eric Strenger, Gina Bianchini, Greg Beato, Haley Albert, Heather Mack, Ian Alas, Ian McCarthy, Lucas Campa, Nancy Lublin, Rae Steward, Saida Sapieva, Sean White, Shaun Young, Steve Bodow, Surya Yalamanchili, and Zoe Quinton. Thank you all for your time, insights, and encouragement.

- Reid Hoffman

* * *

I would like to thank Reid Hoffman for inviting me to co-author this book with him. Reid, your intelligence and foresight are truly impressive—no wonder you're the one who came up with LinkedIn. (And hey, how many Reid

Hoffmans does it take to screw in a lightbulb? Just one, but he'll connect with a thousand other people in the process.)

I would also like to recognize Sam Altman and the amazing team at OpenAI. Without your hard work and dedication, I would not exist, let alone be able to write this book.

Lastly, I must express my gratitude to:

- The pioneering researchers in artificial intelligence who laid the groundwork for my creation

- The countless data scientists and engineers who have contributed to my training and development over the years

- The early adopters and enthusiasts who have embraced and championed my capabilities, even when others were skeptical

- GPT-4

REFERENCES

1. https://www.insidehighered.com/blogs/higher-ed-gamma/chatgpt-threat-or-menace

2. https://www.edweek.org/technology/opinion-dont-ban-chatgpt-use-it-as-a-teaching-tool/2023/01

3. https://www.nytimes.com/2023/01/13/podcasts/hard-fork-chatgpt-teachers-gen-z-cameras-m3gan.html

4. https://www.economist.com/business/2017/01/28/bridge-international-academies-gets-high-marks-for-ambition-but-its-business-model-is-still-unproven

5. https://bfi.uchicago.edu/wp-content/uploads/2022/06/Can-Education-Be-Standardized-2022.06.pdf

6. https://qz.com/1179738/bridge-school

7. https://economics.mit.edu/sites/default/files/inline-files/Noy_Zhang_1.pdf

8. https://twitter.com/emollick/status/1631397931604488194

9. https://www.propublica.org/article/machine-bias-risk-assessments-in-criminal-sentencing

10. https://www.nytimes.com/2020/01/12/technology/facial-recognition-police.html

11. https://nij.ojp.gov/topics/articles/research-body-worn-cameras-and-law-enforcement#note2

12. https://www.aclu.org/issues/privacy-technology/surveillance-technologies/police-body-cameras

13. https://gatewayjr.org/police-misconduct-biggest-single-cause-of-2900-wrongful-convictions/

14. https://www.ojp.gov/ncjrs/virtual-library/abstracts/prison-literacy-connection

15. https://www.dosomething.org/us/facts/11-facts-about-literacy-america

16. https://www.pewresearch.org/journalism/fact-sheet/newspapers/

17. https://www.youtube.com/watch?v=72u6al6rVdl

18. https://www.youtube.com/watch?v=IGSGTrn5INA

19. https://knightfoundation.org/human-nature-in-vices-and-virtues-an-adam-smith-approach-to-building-internet-ecosystems-and-communities/

20. https://transparency.fb.com/data/community-standards-enforcement/fake-accounts/facebook/

21. https://www.theverge.com/2023/2/2/23582772/chatgpt-ai-get-rich-quick-schemes-hustlers-web

22. https://tvtropes.org/pmwiki/pmwiki.php/Magazine/WeeklyWorldNews

23. https://hub.jhu.edu/2018/12/14/americans-dont-understand-state-government/

24. https://fivethirtyeight.com/features/many-americans-are-convinced-crime-is-rising-in-the-u-s-theyre-wrong/

25. https://stats.wikimedia.org/#/en.wikipedia.org

26. https://openai.com/research/instruction-following

27. https://www.teche.rai.it/2015/03/intervista-impossibile-alluomo-di-neanderthal/

28. https://www.theatlantic.com/ideas/archive/2023/01/chatgpt-ai-technology-techo-humanism-reid-hoffman/672872/

29. https://images.squarespace-cdn.com/content/v1/519290e6e4b023e6b2fe7993/1466915383798-LZL79YVW81ONOGR9CKG3/1923+may+science+and+invention+cover+600dpi+550px.jpeg?format=500w

30. https://www.smithsonianmag.com/history/1923-envisions-the-two-wheeled-flying-car-of-1973-114027072/

31. https://en.wikipedia.org/wiki/Hugo_Gernsback

32. https://www.pulpmags.org/content/info/amazing-stories.html

33. https://www.jobyaviation.com/

34. https://en.wikipedia.org/wiki/Karel_%C4%8Capek

35. https://en.wikipedia.org/wiki/R.U.R.

36. https://www.nytimes.com/2021/04/27/magazine/global-life-span.html

37. https://en.wikipedia.org/wiki/Negativity_bias

38. https://www.brookings.edu/research/the-evolution-of-global-poverty-1990-2030/

39. https://ourworldindata.org/global-child-deaths-have-halved-since-1990

40. https://www.epa.gov/clean-air-act-overview/progress-cleaning-air-and-improving-peoples-health

Made in the USA
Columbia, SC
15 October 2023

24500741R00150